GRANT & AT

CW00554629

WHY TAKE FINANCIAL ADVICE?

I HOPE YOU ENJOY MY BOOK,

VERY BEST WISHES,

HOWARD MC.

JUNE 2022

Chartered
Financial
Planner

SOLLA
Society of Later
Life Advisers
ACCREDITED

"Howard's book provides concise and clear advice based on almost 40 years of practical experience within the financial sector.

He provides a broad understanding of where and how money can be invested as well as giving you basic investment rules. He demystifies some of the complex jargon that can confuse those looking to invest and uses some great real-life case studies to illustrate his points.

A well-written, invaluable guide to how to grow your wealth – and pass it on to your loved ones!"
– Rob Lawson OBE, PR and Media Consultant

"The subject of financial planning can be a labyrinth of complexity. In response, the author has drawn upon his 39 years of financial exposure to carefully craft a much-needed text to the market. Chapter by chapter the author dispels such ambiguity in providing clarity, to help readers comprehend the importance of personal financial planning and the key functions to help make informed decisions."
– Dr Derek Watson, Associate Professor, Faculty of Business, Law & Tourism, University of Sunderland

"Howard provides information that is simple and straight-forward but, most importantly, very, very useful.

Furthermore, it can be applied to everyday life and includes examples and instructions that everyone can relate to, inspiring readers to achieve their financial goals through the implementation of sound advice and wealth habit building."
– Phil Pringle, Business Consultant

"Why Take Financial Advice? is very good at covering all the key elements to help individuals look at them-selves and maybe make some decisions about how you handle life. The examples from Howard's and others' experience bring things to life in a brief but effective way. The book highlights the importance of planning for success and then being able to deal with life's issues within the family. I love the idea of full family planning discussions. Having had a few meetings with Howard and my mum and dad, I have seen real value in what he can bring to the table to aid good plans to be created. Although not all of these ideas have been taken by my parents, the important ones have happened i.e. lasting power of attorney for both and inheritance tax planning."
– David McDonald

"When we first met Howard at a financial seminar some years ago, it was clear he saw his role as more than a financial adviser per se. His sincere and genuine approach was the main reason for us engaging him for a first meeting.

Howard's intention to bespoke the advice to our lives, rather than an 'off-the-shelf package', with ongoing reviews is why he remains our adviser to this day.

His book is an excellent practical guide to the 'world of personal finance' and I thoroughly recommend it – it has Howard's personal stamp all over it!"
– Derek Hall

"A must-read for anyone considering saving and investing for the future. Howard explains the benefits of solid financial planning, from gaining a clear understanding of client needs and risk appetite and using this as the basis to create a clear plan to protect clients and their families in the most tax-efficient way possible to enjoy a stress-free retirement."
– Craig Peterson, Co-Founder and Chief Operating Officer at Growth Capital Ventures

ISBN: 9798422521876

Imprint: Independently published

Copyright 2022, Howard McCain

All views expressed in this book are those of the author and are not intended for use as a definitive guide. No part of this publication may be reproduced or transmitted in any form whatsoever without the written permission of Howard McCain: howard.mccain@icloud.com

This book does not constitute financial advice and the reader should not regard any of the financial information provided herein as a personal recommendation. The advice and strategies contained herein may not be suitable for every situation. It is your responsibility to seek the services of a competent professional if professional assistance is required. Neither the author nor the publisher shall be liable for damages arising herefrom.

This book was produced in collaboration with Write Business Results Limited. For more information on their business book, blog and podcast services, please visit www.writebusinessresults.com or contact the team via info@writebusinessresults.com.

WHY TAKE FINANCIAL ADVICE?

How an Adviser Can Help You Understand,
Grow, Enjoy and Pass on Your Wealth

HOWARD McCAIN

Acknowledgements

"The only way to be truly satisfied is to do what you believe is great work. And the only way to do great work is to love what you do. If you haven't found it yet, keep looking. Don't settle. As with all matters of the heart, you'll know when you find it."

— Steve Jobs[1]

Since starting my financial services career in October 1982 with NatWest Bank in South Shields, I have been fortunate to work with some excellent people. Some stand above others, however, as they have either believed in me, inspired me, supported and helped me and remained loyal or they are people who I have learnt the most from.

At NatWest, I would like to thank Peter Marshall who gave me another chance when others had given up on me; Barry Latham who gave me my first opportunity as a financial adviser in 1992; and Mike Edbrooke, Alan Stutt, David Stoddart, Paul Wears, Dave Hulley, Nigel Gregg, Tim Firth, Ian Margerison, Duncan Maw, David Pyle, Chris Honeyman and Kim Wear.

1 Steve Jobs, (2015), Commencement address delivered at Stanford University, 12 June, full text available at: https://news.stanford.edu/2005/06/14/jobs-061505/

My valued clients of St. James's Place (SJP) – thank you for trusting me since 2004 and for continuing to do so.

Richard Balmforth who explained the SJP opportunity in 2003, Phil Pringle, who helped with Nepal 2017/18, and thanks go also to my colleagues in SJP Newcastle location, where our Nepalese fundraising resulted in two schools being built near Kathmandu.

My team at Howard McCain Wealth Associates (HMWA), who helped and supported me from 2004–2020, especially Karen Maddison, Karen Mole, Cameron Finn and Kevin Walker. Also at HMWA, SJP partners George Barker, Stephen Hope, David Atkinson, Grant Callander, Paul Hauxwell, Mark Nield and Karl and Aimee Watson, who have helped to take care of a number of our valued clients since 2012.

Fredaric Bernardin, Jonathan Green, Garth Thompson, Michael Blunt, Michael Sage, Michael Kyle, David Lilley, Ian Price, Peter Grieves, Mike Collins, Rachael Bell, James Richfield, Jon Ellis, David Carrick and Mark Beverley, colleagues at SJP.

The Strategic Coach® Program.

Georgia Kirke of Write Business Results who first planted the book's idea in my mind in 2016.

Charles Mardon, Paul Hursthouse, Danny George, Sarah Jordan and Joanne Atkinson of Sovereign Wealth/SJP.

My valued client introducers since 2004:
Stephen Fletcher, Charles Brewster, Reg Comrie, Leah Hamilton, Paul Hampton, Phil Brown and George Turnbull.

My friends Neil Kirtley, Graham Sleep, Neil Cook, Keith Roberts, Stuart and Tracy Kingsley, Jon Evans, Neil Wilkinson, Kevin Dryden, Gary Watson, David Snowdon, Joe Miller, Tony Watson, Gary Anderson, Mike Hampshire, István Soos, Graeme Barella and Will McCallum.

Two work colleagues stand out, however, for my special acknowledgement and thanks:

My friend Patrick McLaughlin – we built an outstanding investment seminar programme together, delivering hundreds of client events across the North East and Cumbria.

Victoria Curry is my colleague and friend. Vicky is a unique lady who shares my passion for hard work and client service – thank you, Vicky, for your continued loyalty, help, support, energy and inspiration.

Finally, my biggest thanks of all are for my wife, Gill – a truly "Special Lady" – well done for putting up with me for the last 30 years and here is to our next 40 plus together. Yes, you are right – I am a lucky man.

To Gill, Alex and Euan.

Contents

Foreword

I have just finished reading Howard's book and it has been so refreshing to see someone decide to write about financial advice and the benefits that financial advice can bring you and your family. I have been in financial services all my working life, starting way back in 1977 for Hambro Life in Swindon. The one thing that has been constant in this time is all the changes that have taken place within financial services.

What Howard has done is break areas down into bite-size chunks and explain in detail with great examples what you should consider and also what you should look out for. Using his own personal experience really brings home the importance of advice. He highlights what to do, how important it is to pick the right adviser for you and your family and how understanding invest-ments will make a real difference.

We know that a lot of us do not spend enough time looking at our finances; reading this book gives you a great insight into what you might need to do and consider.

I started working at St. James's Place in 2004, the same time that Howard decided to also move there. I have been lucky enough to know and work with Howard. He realised very quickly that getting as many qualifications as possible was going to be key going forward. Howard always puts his clients first, explaining what advice he is giving and why he is giving that advice. He has a unique way of using his own life experiences to again explain what to do and what not to do.

I know that Howard still gets a real buzz out of helping people achieve their financial goals; as you can see, he also wants to help others by writing this book.

I would suggest that the time reading this book will be well spent.

Ian Price

Director, Price Consultancy and former Divisional Director, Pensions & Consultancy at St. James's Place Wealth Management

Introduction

This book is designed to give you the answers to all the initial questions you have about estate planning, wealth management, investing and financial planning, but didn't know who to ask. I want to cut through this ever-complicated financial world with clear and easy-to-understand descriptions of what broad financial products and services a financial planner can utilise to your advantage. I also want to give you a "glimpse under the bonnet" of the journey to constructing a bespoke client financial planning recommendation without you having to get your hands dirty by taking the time and qualifications necessary to do so.

This book's purpose is also to help you decide whether or not to engage a financial planner to help you through your journey and to share the advantages you will gain if you decide to do so.

In some cases, I may answer questions you also didn't know to ask. In my experience, there can be a great deal of confusion within the fields of protection, investment, pensions, inheritance tax, will provision and the like. What I aim to do in the following chapters is share my knowledge about the various aspects of financial planning that I believe everyone should be aware of, including elements that both the first-time investor and the more seasoned investor can understand and take something away from.

This is not intended as a guide so that you can do your own financial and estate planning without the support of qualified professionals. Rather, my intention is to give you a base level of knowledge so that you can understand what you might require from a financial planner and, most importantly, why. That said, if you have a simplistic overall estate set up, or you enjoy managing your own investment estate affairs without professional help and are prepared to put in the "hard yards" required, you may, having read this book, be able to do it all yourself. I will not be seeking to "sell" you financial planner engagement; rather, I simply want to put you in a position whereby you can make a clear and informed choice as to whether or not to engage.

That said, an experienced and well-qualified financial planner is worth their weight in gold. I would recommend you seek out a chartered financial planner, who are among the most highly qualified professionals in the industry. Achieving chartered status takes years of experience and dedication to focused knowledge. Therefore, achieving chartered status differentiates those who have gone the extra mile and, as a result, are more likely to go the extra mile for their clients.

As you'll discover in the first chapter, their role encompasses three key areas, namely, advice, service and performance. When you are looking for a financial planner, you want to find someone who brings these three elements together, ensuring not only that your wealth is in safe hands but that you find a professional who wants to get to know you as a person and develop a long-term, trusted relationship that will be to the benefit of both of you.

This is about taking a holistic view of your life and putting you firmly at the centre of any plan that we create. A good financial adviser will do more than simply focus on your finances; they will act as a trusted mentor and coach to understand your goals in life and then provide the leadership and guidance you need to achieve those goals.

If you have picked up this book, chances are that you're interested in financial planning and can see that it could be of benefit to you. By the time you finish this book, I want you to have a comprehensive understanding of the high levels of advice and service an excellent financial adviser can provide you with, as well as the other professionals who can support you in related areas, such as will writing and later life care.

I also want you to understand investments and how they can benefit your financial future when aligned to sound financial advice and service.

I want you to have a broad understanding of where money can be invested, as well as how, by following a few fairly basic investment rules, you can both grow it and enjoy it best during your lifetime. I also want you to understand how to pass this money on to your loved ones in the way you desire, as tax efficiently and seamlessly as possible.

A whole-life view

I have worked in financial services for over 39 years and have helped hundreds of people and their families secure their financial futures. My role as a chartered financial planner is not only to advise you on financial matters but also to make sure that you lay the necessary foundations for a strong financial plan and therefore a financially independent future.

I believe a good financial planner should know about every key element of their clients' lives that relates to their long-term financial plan. I want to know where you have been, where you are now and what hopes, dreams and goals you have for the future. Only by getting to know you as a person can I provide the levels of advice and service I pride myself and my firm on.

Financial planning is certainly not all about the money. There are many factors that can influence your financial plan and many things that need to be in place before we begin to map out your future. Wills, lasting power of attorney (LPA) and intergenerational succession planning are the cornerstones of a good financial plan. Understanding your existing investments and the products recommended to you is essential for building a lasting and trusting relationship with your adviser.

My aim is to not only give my clients peace of mind that they will never run out of money but also show them that their loved ones will be taken care of when they pass away. Intergenerational advice

is an important part of my work, and I
believe engaging with the next generation
is just as vital as supporting my clients
because they will be the beneficiaries
of plans I put in place just as my clients
will. Intergenerational advice can also
involve supporting your parents as
they navigate the later stages of their
life to ensure that they are well taken
care of both financially and in terms of
any other support they may require.

In Part 1 of this book, I explain what I
believe are the three essential elements
that should make up a financial planner's
offering advice, service and performance.
I also share my seven golden rules for
investing, and if you follow these rules
throughout your life's financial journey I
believe that you can't go too far wrong.

In Part 2, I give you an outline of the most
important aspects of estate planning,
focusing on all the things you need to put
in place to ensure that not only you but
also your family are well protected. This

is where we consider the legacy you will leave behind, not only financially but also in terms of how your affairs are organised. Some of what I share here – such as in relation to wills, later life advice and pensions – will be applicable regardless of your circumstances. Other elements I discuss, such as inheritance tax, personal protection and investment options, may not apply to everyone; take what you need from these chapters and leave the rest.

Finally, in Part 3 I look at how we can create your financial plan and what your financial support network can look like. You will notice as you move through the book that I strongly recommend engaging professionals in particular specialisms and it is these trusted advisers who form your network. Your financial planner is just one of these professionals, but they are ideally placed to connect you to professionals who can not only provide the services and advice you need, but who will do so to the same high standard.

Throughout the book I have shared a number of real-life client scenarios where I have set out my perception of how I have helped my clients, with their specific feedback also replayed as to how my advice has impacted their lives so that you can see the practical effect of the theory.

Let's start by exploring investment and, more specifically, how those three pillars of advice, service and performance work together.

Part 1:

Simplifying Investment (Understand It and Grow It)

In this first part of the book, I want to give you a basic level of understanding about what you can and should expect from a well-qualified and experienced financial planner. As I explained in the introduction, this means understanding how the three pillars of advice, service and performance come together to serve your and your family's best interests. I term these "the three expectations" because I believe it is reasonable for you, as a client, to expect all three from any financial planner or other professional you engage.

While these three expectations are important regardless of why you have engaged a financial planner, they are particularly important in relation to investment. If, like many other people, you have limited knowledge about different forms of investment, you will likely be looking for advice about the most appropriate route for you. This advice will need to take into account your individual circumstances, your tolerance for risk, the timescale you are working to and what level of return you hope to gain.

When you engage a financial planner to help you manage your investments, you want to know they are available should you have any questions or concerns.

The level of service they provide is therefore essential to give you peace of mind and make your life as easy as possible. You will, of course, also want your investments to perform well and this is why the third of those expectations is important. To truly make the most of your investments and your financial planning in general, you need all three of those elements to work together.

In Chapter 2, I will explain my seven golden rules that I believe are the cornerstones of good investment. If you follow these rules, you can't go too far wrong, even at times of market volatility. These two chapters will give you a thorough introduction to, and a solid understanding of, financial planning and how it can help you specifically in relation to investing.

Chapter 1:

The Three Expectations

"Money isn't the most important thing in life, but it's reasonably close to oxygen on the 'gotta have it' scale."

– Zig Ziglar

There are three elements to financial planning that are inextricably linked and each is just as important as the others. These are advice, service and performance. In my experience, it is common for clients to focus on just one of these elements in isolation, usually performance, believing that they can do the rest themselves. However, as you'll learn in this chapter, it is the combination of all three of these elements that sets the best financial planners apart from the rest.

Let's explore each of these elements in turn before looking at how they all feed into one another.

Advice

As a chartered financial planner, advice only comes into play once I have thoroughly got to know each client. This requires a detailed investigation of your past, present and future because first of all I need to understand where you are precisely in your life and then explore where exactly you want to head in order to help me devise the right financial plan to help you get there. There are two threads to the advice I provide. The first is the initial planning advice I will give once I have got to know you, your goals and your current situation. The second is the ongoing advice I provide to ensure that your financial plan is continually working as it should.

The advice element is where my expertise and experience in financial services comes in because I have put in both the time and the hard yards to understand what the financial advisory industry can offer the client. There are three broad areas that my advice covers: the first is protection, the second is pension provision and the third is investments and savings. In addition, an area I do not advise upon, but that nonetheless is equally important, is robust will provision, as well as having an LPA in place.

Protection comes first because it's important to make sure that you are fully protected in the event of death, critical illness or incapacity and that this protection ties in with your longer-term retirement, investment and savings goals. Once sufficient protection is in place and you are completely content with it, we can explore the other two elements of your financial plan.

It's also important to recognise that advice is a two-way street. It's crucial that you, as a client, are transparent, open and that you fully engage. It is also essential that you follow through on recommended advice actions within this process. This will enable your financial planner to give you the best possible advice, as they will fully understand your circumstances and know that you will follow through on the advice actions recommended.

When it comes to giving advice, it's my job to make sure that you understand what I'm advising you to do and why, because the next stage after you receive advice is for you to take action off the back of it – and you are much more likely to do this if you fully understand my recommendations. Just like the advice, which is broken down into initial and ongoing, your actions will be the same. Some of the steps you will be advised to take may not have an impact for years, or in some cases even generations, to come. As a result, I don't only see the client as the person who is sitting in front of me but as their whole extended family because what I recommend may well impact future generations.

I am talking about providing intergenerational advice, which holds a great deal of value because it ensures that the children and even grandchildren of my clients understand how their wealth is being managed and how that will affect them. This is also where protecting your wealth comes in, so that you are able to pass it on in the most tax-efficient way possible.

Advice is fundamental to financial planning and wealth management because this is where the change happens and the catalyst for that change comes from each of my clients being able to see how the concepts I am talking about can affect their lives.

My role is to bring my advice to life for you and show you where you may decide to make life-changing decisions. Often these are decisions you may never have considered before. For example, I had a client in Cumbria who was separated from her husband. He was paying her a monthly amount by way of a private arrangement, so I asked my client the question: "What would happen to this much-required monthly payment if he were to pass away?" Of course, the answer was that it would cease. The outcome in this instance was that divorce proceedings commenced and, upon completion, my client received a pension sharing order for a proportion of his pension so that the monthly private arrangement was not only guaranteed for the rest of her life but also indexed upwards annually in line with inflation.

Another example could be that you're in your 30s with a large mortgage and a family, so taking out a life and critical illness plan to cover the mortgage loan, as well as a life cover plan to protect your family in the event of death, is recommended. A further consideration is what happens if you cannot work due to sickness or injury? Let's say you are earning £50,000 per annum. If you are employed then typically you may receive up to one year of replacement income from a caring employer, but what will happen after that? State benefits are limited so taking out an income replacement plan matched to your retirement age, which provides a tax-free benefit in addition to state benefits, may be the recommended solution.

It has always amazed me that we are all keen to comprehensively insure our car, house and beloved family pet, yet when it comes to covering our own lives and incomes I have often heard the cry: "We don't believe in insurance!"

Take the example of the client earning £50,000 per annum. Each year £50,000 rolls into their bank account, but let's imagine that instead of the person earning the money, it was a "money machine" at the bottom of their garden churning out £50,000 year in, year out. Would you insure this machine in case it broke down or was stolen? Of course you would! And yet a number of us are reluctant to insure our own money machine (which is our life) and yet we happily renew our car insurance (which is required by law) year in and year out. So, personal protection is vital and comes before the "nicer" things like saving for retirement – remember if you do not have adequate protection in place will you even be able to save for a comfortable retirement?

The long-term benefits of adequate protection

At the age of 39, Henry had a heart attack. Although it was fairly mild, he was signed off work and he was never well enough to work again in his same employment. Henry had taken out, via a financial adviser (not myself – I had not met him then), an income replacement plan, which meant he then received a tax-free monthly benefit after the deferred period had elapsed until he either was well enough to work in his job again OR the expiry age of the plan, which was age 65.

I met him in his early 60s and he had been receiving this private income replacement benefit since he had his heart attack at age 39. He had had a happy and healthy life thus far and, because of the income replacement plan, he and his family had never had financial worries since his heart attack.

Had he not had the foresight to put the plan in place, the story would likely have been very different. Henry was well thought of and well-liked at the company he used to work for, but they would not have been able to afford to continue paying him over the long term. At some point, they would have moved him to standard statutory sick pay and that would have put him and his family in a very difficult financial situation. Income replacement bene-fited him by allowing him to stay out of work and focus on staying healthy and continuing to save for his retirement, which, happily, he is now enjoying. I am also helping him and his wife with investment and pension decumula-tion advice – the advice he took many years ago changed their lives.

I am passionate about ensuring that each of my clients has adequate protection in place so that they can sleep at night and I do this by fully informing them across the areas they can protect so that they can make that informed choice. Protection cover and products are typically inexpensive – often for less than the price of a Saturday night weekly takeaway a client can protect their loved ones' financial futures.

Pensions and savings are another area where I regularly advise clients. One of the most common situations I encounter is one where someone has been putting money into their pension each month without understanding what that amount will achieve in real terms for them in retirement or having a specific goal in mind. In this situation, the advice has to be specific, factoring in when they will retire, how much they want to live on in retirement, their current provisions and likely state pension benefits – clients typically want to know when they can become financially independent so that they have life choices.

Everyone's "golden number" for financial independence is different and the job of the financial planner is to carefully find out yours. I cover investment advice in Chapter 2 when I explain the seven golden rules. Once protection and pensions are covered though, my broad advice is to "keep enough money in cash accounts but not too much and invest the rest" – more on this later.

Inheritance tax planning is a specialist and bespoke advice area requiring not only the financial planner's advice but also the input of a top-quality solicitor/will writer. It is when the advice of these professionals is provided in tandem with financial advice that an invaluable client outcome can be achieved. Inheritance tax mitigation advice is usually required in stages and I think it is important to adopt a staggered and measured long-term approach, ideally engaging will executors, trustees and beneficiaries rather than adopting a "one-off only, sledgehammer" advice approach. The earlier we start inheritance tax mitigation, the better, and keeping accurate records of investments and gifts made is vital. This is not only about helping your estate save what can amount to hundreds of thousands of pounds but, more importantly, about ensuring that when you do pass away your estate can be passed on without months of worry and insecurity for the executors and beneficiaries as it seamlessly passes through probate.

I also want to mention that the provision of financial advice should be given to all parties affected by the advice. So, for example, if I am advising a married couple or a registered civil partnership I want to see and advise both parties, not just one of them.

In each of these situations, my advice can not only help you to protect your wealth but also give you and your family long-term peace of mind. Again, we see the intergenerational theme emerging.

It is also important to be aware of the concept of guaranteed advice. We are only human and all of us can make mistakes (especially me!). Choosing a provider who is backed by a strong parent firm will provide you with further reassurance should a financial adviser make a mistake when providing financial advice. I know in this situation the parent firm I represent will investigate and seek to rectify any issues, this is because they stand in the shoes of their adviser representative and understand the importance of providing suitable advice/recommendations for each individual client circumstance.

Before you engage a financial adviser, ask what advice guarantees their firm has in place (over and above the standard financial regulatory ones) and how their complaints procedure operates. Any adviser who says they NEVER make a mistake should be viewed with caution; therefore, make sure the adviser you appoint has a good firm behind them safeguarding the advice you are given.

Service

The next of the three core elements to financial planning is service. In the UK's financial services industry, in my opinion, the service is typically (at best) poor. Often clients are left hanging by financial service providers and they have to chase for things to get done or spend time on hold or in queues to be heard or seen. I believe the reason for this is that there is no clarity over who has ultimate responsibility for delivering outstanding service to clients and in helping them with their ongoing transactional needs.

Service covers every part of your journey, from the accumulation stage where you create a financial plan to the products you purchase and ensuring that both the products themselves and the providers are effective to help you follow that plan.

As a financial planner, my role is to not only recommend products and providers but also to ensure that they follow through and deliver on what you require. As a client, you want to work with a firm that has team members, as well as advisers, who are committed to delivering good service and who respond to your queries in a timely and understanding manner. This extends to helping you with everything from getting a state pension forecast from HMRC to using our online investment valuation platform, as well as the experience you have when you visit the office for an in-person meeting. For me, service is about providing you with the reassurance and safety blanket of a local phone number that you can ring, where you know whoever you speak to will be committed to supporting you.

When it comes to service from a financial planner, you want to know that their team is just as committed to delivering exceptional service as the planner is because they will ensure that you get what you need both from them and from any other providers you engage with.

In meeting a client for the first time, they will typically find out that the client has bought a number of financial products either from banks, building societies, insurance companies and previous financial advisers or directly themselves using an online pension or investment platform. The problem often occurs when this client needs to speak to the product provider about accessing their investment or pension or understanding the features and benefits of a life or critical illness plan (how much cover, is the plan in trust, are the premiums guaranteed, what flexibility options are there on, say, moving home, and how perhaps to amend or increase the cover). Here is where the service aspect becomes vital.

Over the years I have seen countless times when a simple term life assurance plan has been taken out by a client to protect their family (either completing the cover themselves or often through another financial adviser) and yet that plan is not written into trust. However, the advantages of writing the plan into trust should it pay out are two-fold: firstly, timely and fast payment to the trustees (who can distribute to the beneficiaries) without having to go through probate and, secondly, the plan falls outside of the client's estate, potentially saving 40 per cent inheritance tax on the proceeds. Quite simply, the plan can be added to trust, at no cost to the client, usually appointing family members as trustees and beneficiaries with an expression of wish letter added so that the client explains to the trustees precisely what they want to happen should they die during the term.

My advice to a client is to not only choose your financial adviser in terms of the advice and product performance they will recommend but also ask them how their firm (back office staff locally) will take full responsibility for service – such that all of their existing provider products and services have a local contact point who can save the client valuable time. Typically, my clients give us authority so that we can contact all of their existing product providers. This means when I see them I can not only present updates for our own product features and performance, but I can also report upon their externally held products and plans, saving my client valuable time.

Another key element of service is communication and explaining when a process might take a little longer, structuring your service delivery expectations, because of factors outside of our control. Providing you with a timeline reassures you that action is being taken and gives you that all-important peace of mind.

Let me share my best example of outstanding client service. I like Apple products and visiting my local Apple store. When I arrive, I am seen straight away by a knowledgeable person who knows the product I am buying inside out and explains how it works to a technophobe like myself. I will typically take in my old iPhone or iPad and swap it for the latest model, having received some coaching on the new features. I might also sign up for a face-to-face or remote tutorial to improve my IT skills. I walk out feeling I have a better product that I know how to use and, if something went wrong with it, where to go for help.

I want to replicate this level of service when a financial planning client appoints me as their long-term adviser.

Finally, I believe that great service when dealing with a financial adviser means the firm and adviser taking responsibility for complete client care. This is a firm where all staff care about the client and are prepared to walk the "extra mile" to contact and obtain, for example, the right information about their existing plans so that a client is never allowed to be "left hanging". With a firm like this, the client also has a local access point to staff who they know, like and, very importantly, trust.

Performance

The final one of the three essential elements is performance, which refers to the performance of the underlying investment or pension plan. We might compare performance against the returns you can obtain on cash accounts, or in the UK we often compare investment performance to the FTSE 100, which is the basket of the largest companies in the UK. When it comes to investment performance, there is a correlation to investment risk and this is where, as the adviser, it is my role to ensure you thoroughly understand risk from all elements, ranging from cash through to individual equities and everything in between.

Each person's tolerance for investment risk is different. That will affect which products they already have, as well as what they are prepared to invest in moving forward. When I meet a client, I always want to understand what investments they currently have, why they bought them, from whom and importantly whether they fully understand the products' features, risk and volatility position and how they will impact upon their financial plan. This applies whether it's a defined contribution (DC) pension, ISAs, unit trust, investment trusts, structured products, cash accounts and bonds or investment bonds.

Once I understand this, I will be able to explain what risk you are currently taking and can put that into the context of your longer-term goals. Keeping what you want to achieve in mind is vital when it comes to looking at the performance of your investments because you need to know that each of these products is delivering what you need it to and, if it isn't, then you need to explore your other options.

Advice and service are very closely linked to performance because it is my role to explain investments (and any associated risks) to each of my clients and to provide them with advice about how they can best manage their portfolio to achieve their goals. If you, as a client, are only interested in performance and are not interested in advice or service, then I would question whether a chartered financial planner is the right person to be engaging with. You will likely find an advisory stockbroker is a better option if you are only interested in performance, or that you may be better served by selecting investment products yourself via an online platform – but please remember that this latter option is fraught with danger. How does an amateur investor know which are the best funds/investments to select and monitor and then change them when the requisite performance levels are not happening?

In the next chapter, I'll share my seven golden rules of investment that will explore various aspects of investment and performance in much greater detail.

A note on fund management

Before we get to those rules, I would like to take some time to explain how fund management works, what exactly a fund manager is and the role they conduct. You may already be a seasoned investor and therefore you may wish to skip the following few paragraphs or, as a new or first-time investor, this description should prove helpful. Either way, it is important to apply the concepts of advice, service and performance to fund managers as well as to financial advisers.

A fund manager is typically a person who is based in one of the world's major financial centres (London/ Paris/New York/Los Angeles) and they (and their fund management team) simply manage a "pool" of client money. When you buy into a fund, your money as an individual client will be pooled with that of many other clients and you buy units in that "pooled" fund, whether it be a pension fund, investment bond or a unit trust fund wrapped in or outside of an ISA umbrella. A typical fund can have a value of up to £1 billion – and as, say, an annual ISA investor your, for example, £20,000 investment simply buys "units" and therefore a small proportion of this £1 billion fund.

The price of the units you have bought with your £20,000 will fluctuate daily and the unit price will fare as well or as badly as the reported daily price of the fund. Therefore, it is very important that your chosen fund manager, who is making the decisions about which assets within the fund to buy, hold and sell, is "on the ball" and acts with due skill, care and diligence. It would also be good if your chosen manager had investment flair, knowledge and know-how – in fact, you want to have the very best person and investment team in charge of your hard-earned money, who are going to maximise returns for you.

This all means you are not only buying units of that fund, but you are also selecting the fund manager. Of course, you want to know that they are at, and will remain at, the very top of their field within the asset class you are investing in. These asset classes will typically be shares/equities, fixed interest (gilts/corporate bonds), commercial property/infrastructure or alternative investments such as gold, silver, tin, copper, wheat or minerals.

Let's think about it – money can largely only be invested within these aforementioned asset classes (as well as residential property). A fund manager will usually have a team of analysts, maybe upwards of 20 people strong. Let's say we are talking about a UK equity/share fund. That fund manager's job is to select the right UK shares at the right time, holding for sale and/or re-purchase at the right time to ensure the fund value goes upwards. A diligent fund management team will carry out detailed research, not simply desk based, by visiting the companies they are investing in and carrying out thorough due diligence before choosing to invest. They will then regularly follow up those real-life discussions. A good fund manager will carry out many of these company meetings themselves and will have an excellent research team supporting them, which will enable them to make good longer-term investment decisions and to seek growth and value opportunities (rolling advice, service and performance into one package).

Again, let's think about it: what would you prefer? A desktop research fund manager relying on statistical models and following the latest fad or fashionable share based upon a well-known market trend to select their investments OR a fund manager who makes judicious investment decisions by comprehensively seeking out those companies who are perhaps "under the radar" and conducting thorough and detailed research along with an examination/knowledge of their management team and balance sheet/long-terms plans of the company?

Sadly there are, naturally, some active fund managers who don't carry out this level of research and who aren't as proactive. They might simply buy and hold a basket of top FTSE 100 shares without undertaking the necessary due diligence – the question is, are these active fund managers really adding value for their fee or would a client be better served within a cheaper, passively managed fund? This is why choosing the right fund manager is so important.

The difference between active and passive fund manage-ment is worth a brief description here too. Active fund managers will have a "live" portfolio of their asset class where they are continually making investment decisions as to what holdings to buy and sell and at what time. For this extra due diligence, you will typically see their fees are higher than a passively managed fund. The active manager, however, seeks to "earn their fee" by beating their benchmark passive market indices by, for example, finding growth and value companies which will increase in value longer term. Knowing when to buy, hold and sell these companies takes flair and skill to ensure value results for the fund.

By contrast, a passive fund manager will typically seek to "mirror" financial market indices with their under-lying share holdings – say the FTSE 100, 350, MSCI, NASDAQ or the DOW – in the hope that, longer term, the whole market (and therefore the indices they are linked to) moves upwards. The passive element means that they cannot influence individual holdings nor take advantage of niche or individual share-buying opportunities. Their fees will usually be cheaper as they are not undertaking this research or active in the buy/hold/sell positions – once their portfolio mirrors the indices, they simply amend any company index changes remotely.

An example share in the FTSE 100 is Rolls Royce Holdings PLC (RR). In the calendar year of 2021, RR had a high price of £1.50 and a low price of 87p. If a shrewd active manager had bought RR close to its low price in 2021 and sold close to its high price then a strong profit would of course materialise – this trade is simply not possible with a passively managed fund. There is too much talk in investment circles of the great benefits of cheaply managed passive funds versus their more expensive active counterparts in my opinion – my one rider to this is that your chosen active managers need to be the very best available.

Passively managed funds can also be highly volatile and arguably lack diversification. Take the US DOW or NASDAQ indices: they comprise disproportionately large holdings in the FAANG top five shares/stocks – Facebook (now Meta), Amazon, Apple, Netflix and Google (now Alphabet) – which the passive investor is exposed to. It is also worth remembering that on 2 August 2018 Apple became the world's first $1 trillion market cap company and on 3 January 2022 it became the world's first $3 trillion company. The passive investor therefore takes on an ever greater exposure to the Apple stock, which narrows their investment diversification. The story is similar for the other big four FAANG shares that have seen huge growth in a short space of time. Can this huge growth continue or will the bubble burst?

When it does, the passive investor has a greater diversification risk in my mind than the widely diversified, actively invested portfolio fund client.

The difficulty a client has is knowing:

- Which active managers are good and which ones are poor?

- How to ensure that a good active manager, once appointed, is consistently performing at the top of their game? What if they are about to retire? What if a key analyst or stock selector moves on?

The job of a fund manager is very important, which is why it's so important to find the very best fund managers who will make considered investment decisions with your hard-earned money so that, in the longer term, your money will perform well. This is something we'll come back to when we get to rule number six in my golden rules of investment in the next chapter.

Some actively managed funds have a small passively managed element within them and I think that a small element of passivity is the right fit for a balanced investment portfolio. Therefore, passive management does have its place as part of a widely diversified portfolio.

Risk and reward

One of my roles as an adviser is to help my clients (and now you) understand what risk means for your investment and how, by diversifying across all asset classes (cash, fixed interest, shares, property, alternatives and infrastructure), you can not only bring risk and volatility down but also achieve inflation-beating returns.

I have often spoken to clients who are comparing a high-risk, highly volatile product with one that carries a much lower risk and lower volatility and who are then under the false impression that the high-risk product is the better of the two. This is often because it has performed better in the shorter (two to five year) term. This will usually be when share/equity markets have performed strongly. Of course, this will be true – a plan invested solely in, for example, UK shares will almost definitely perform better in the shorter term when the FTSE 100 has performed well against a lower risk diversified unit trust fund which is invested across all of the asset classes previously described. However, it is my job to explain to the client that often they are not comparing like for like.

This is all about helping you to understand that if you are going to accept additional risk, you must also accept additional volatility because the two go hand-in-hand. I will also help you understand the difference between active and passive fund management and the risks and rewards of each approach. At my firm, we largely (but not exclusively) believe in active fund management, where the best active fund managers work across well-diversified portfolios of investments that are either cautious, medium-range or slightly more adventurous in their risk profiles, to ensure your investments are continually performing at their best.

The following diagram is my "pyramid of investment risk". At the apex, therefore, the highest risk levels are individual shares and a share portfolio, followed by niche and more specialised investment funds (for example, China Special Situations) and later in the book I will explain why they are here. Then come managed funds, which are typically broadly invested across all main asset classes, and finally (and arguably the most secure) a "multi-manager approach" where a number of investment funds form a broad portfolio and mix across all asset classes, diversifying across fund manager styles.

I return to this pyramid in golden rule number four when highlighting investment diversification and in describing the main asset classes, but it is important to remember that if you are an existing investor your current portfolio is likely to be at or scattered around on this pyramid – my role is to show you where you currently are, ask you why and how you got there and, if we need to change your plan, where you end up once we have formulated your plan.

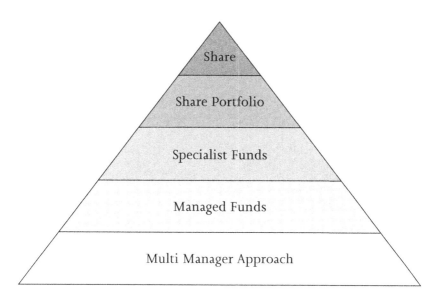

Returning then to active fund management, each active manager is carefully selected and their performance is regularly monitored against specific benchmarks to ensure they are consistently performing well. Active fund management has served my clients incredibly well and, in addition to the strong performance of their investments, they also receive excellent service and advice as standard from myself and my team locally.

Understanding is the key to providing good advice

I always want to do the best I possibly can for each of my clients and the only way for me to provide them with good advice is to fully understand them. When you think about this logically, how can an adviser provide you with good advice if they don't fully and holistically understand you? If you liken this to the medical profession, a doctor can't give the right advice or prescribe the right medication if they haven't thoroughly examined their patient first. It's really no different with financial advice.

As a client, you will find this in the initial engagement you have with a new adviser. What you want to see is someone who is seeking to understand not only your financial life but you as an individual. It might seem simple for an adviser to recommend you set up a pension if you don't already have one, for instance, but this ignores the complexity and nuances of your life. There are a great deal of elements to consider around how a pension fits into your overall financial life and how it links in with your goals.

Poor advice can be devastating to your financial future because it can affect not only whether and when you'll reach retirement but also whether you will be in a position to live the life you want to live when you retire. People pay thousands of pounds for advice that doesn't serve them, but it isn't only the financial cost that concerns me: poor advice can also have a devastating impact on the client and their family, especially if the likes of making a will and an LPA are not discussed and actioned.

I believe that a financial adviser's responsibility is, first and foremost, to make sure that each client is fully protected, which means having sufficient life insurance, as well as critical illness and incapacity benefits. Only once those fundamentals are in place do you look at the other elements of someone's financial life, such as their investments and savings.

Product knowledge is only a (small but essential) part of the picture

My approach is that providing good advice to our clients is 70 per cent about understanding each client and only 30 per cent about my underlying product and industry knowledge. As a chartered professional, it is a given that I understand complex financial products and how they will be of benefit to my clients. This knowledge and experience has been honed over 39 years within the industry, over hundreds of hours of textbook study and the understanding of real-life client scenarios and experiences. I have to continually keep on top of my professional development, be aware of "knowledge fade" and how to address it and be attuned to any changes within the industry.

It's also important to recognise when I am not an expert in a particular area of financial advice and planning and to bring in another qualified professional who is able to help my client in these circumstances. Equity release, mortgage advice and defined benefit (DB) pension advice, for example, are areas I can advise upon but that instead I prefer to refer to close colleagues within my firm to assist my clients.

However, as I mentioned, this detailed product knowledge really does only cover about 30 per cent of what I provide as an adviser. The other 70 per cent of what I do involves getting to know you, putting myself in your shoes and walking around in them and then recommending the right financial planning. If I'm working with a married couple or civil partnership, I have to put myself in both people's shoes so that I can understand them equally, by listening actively to what they both may want. This, to me, is more important than the underlying product/technical knowledge because my role isn't just to provide initial advice and walk away; it's to formulate a plan and constantly revisit it to ensure it is still working in the best interests of each client for the remainder of their lives and also intergenerationally.

Finding the "why" behind the facts

As a financial adviser, part of my role with a new client is to carry out fact finding, which involves firstly uncovering all the "core" details I need to know about you. This includes the basics, like your full name, address, marital status and date of birth, your children's/dependants' names/ages/dates of birth and how long you expect them to be financially dependent upon you, as well as your current health position and smoking status. Fact finding also encompasses all the details around your financial life, including details of your will, fixed and liquid assets, a detailed monthly essential and discretionary expenditure list, liabilities, current pension(s), savings, investments and trust investments and protection plan provisions. Once I have those hard facts, my next job is to bring them to life and I do this by understanding your past and getting to know your future goals, aims and aspirations.

I want to know where you were educated, what your biggest achievement to date is and what your short-, medium- and longer-term goals are. I also like to dig into career history and not only find out what you do for a living, but why. Why did you choose to study a particular subject or go to a certain university? Why did you change your career path? Why did you choose to work for that company? To provide high-quality advice, I want to know why you made those decisions in the past, as well as fully understand where you are now and where you want to head to.

Once I understand you and your life, I want to know about your future, such as when you want to retire and what ambitions you have for your children. I'm particularly interested in learning about each of my clients' children, if they have them, and what stage in their life they are at. I'm a big advocate of financial education from an early age because I think it's incredibly important to engage the next generation with financial advice. To me, this is another important aspect of intergenerational advice that can sadly be overlooked.

On a personal level, I find people fascinating and I love hearing people's life and career stories. Everyone has paddled a different canoe, so to speak, and I enjoy hearing about their journeys to this point in their lives, as well as where they want to go from here. At this stage, my job is to help you achieve what you want to achieve financially. It's as simple as that.

Looking to the future

I ask my clients three simple questions once I have a good understanding of them as people, as well as of their financial lives. These three questions are part of a tool that I learnt from attending The Strategic Coach® Program, called The D.O.S. Conversation®. They are: In the next five, ten and 15 years' time, from a financial perspective, what dangers do you face, what opportunities do you want to build upon and what strengths do you want to maximise?

When it comes to drilling down into the dangers, the conversations are usually around when the client might die and the fallout from this, their health concerns, financial worries and job security. The opportunities are often around building a business, maybe growing a business and taking on new staff, getting married or retiring, depending on where you are on your journey. The kinds of strengths people often cite from a financial perspective are having a solid pension, having substantial savings and investments and having good protection in place, as well as other strengths such as being in good health and excellent physical fitness and a happy and fulfilling marriage or civil partnership.

Once we have the answers to those three key questions, we can work on eliminating the dangers, or at least minimising them, as well as building upon your opportunities and strengths. Often clients will tell me they wish they'd met me ten years ago and, while that might be true, what we have to do is work from where we are now. I can tell you that, with a good and regularly reviewed plan, you can build the future you want and it is never too late to start. As an adviser, it's my role to do this in partnership with you. I find it incredibly rewarding to see people building a plan and then working towards their future goals and aspirations.

The ability to really listen to my clients is incredibly important (the fact we have two ears and just one mouth was a point made to me on my initial training in 1992!).

As I mentioned earlier, I believe engaging with the next generation is just as important as working closely with my clients. In fact, I often feel that my best-served clients are the ones where I have also met their ultimate will beneficiaries, who are usually their children, nieces and nephews or extended family, like siblings, as this is where the wealth is ultimately headed.

Family meetings can typically work very well. Often my clients are mum and dad so when, with their approval, I can meet their ultimate beneficiaries (their children) and have full authority to explain their parents' estate and my advice/future plans, upon first or second death the family all know what will happen from a financial perspective.

This is why it is so important for me to understand your "why" and to gather all of those "soft" facts about your life before we build your plan together. This plan doesn't have to be complicated; in fact, I prefer to adopt the "KISS" principle – "keep it simple, stupid" – and my role along the way is to ensure you benefit from those three essential elements of advice, service and performance, not only during your life but also your future generations' lives.

Summary

The three essential elements of advice, service and performance should form the bedrock of any solid financial advice and recommendations and a long-term financial adviser relationship. Once I have got to know you, by carrying out the kind of thorough fact finding I talked about in this chapter, it actually makes it much easier for me to make appropriate recommendations for your financial future. I can apply my product knowledge and decades of experience in financial services to your "why" and help you build a plan that takes you in the direction you want to move in.

I have to blend carefully tailored and bespoke advice to your own circumstances and your desired investment performance versus the risk you are prepared to take with any underlying investment here, but it is also key that I think about service and that you are given clear service expectations from my support team over the short, medium and longer term.

It's my role to cut through this ever more complex financial world and explain my advice clearly to ensure that you understand the key features and benefits of any products I recommend, as well as being very transparent about the associated fees. I want you to know exactly what you are getting in terms of product and service and that you understand thoroughly the fees you will pay for the service.

It is also important that I work closely with you to continually build upon the initial recommendations I make, to ensure that your financial plan and goals are met longer term. For me, blending and balancing these three elements of advice, service and performance is what good financial planning advice is all about.

Chapter 2:

The Seven Golden Rules
of Investment

"We have two classes for forecasters: those who don't know and those who don't know they don't know."

— John Kenneth Galbraith

The rules I'm going to share with you in this chapter are rules that I've used throughout my career and they are what I believe to be the cornerstones of good investment advice. If you carefully follow these seven golden rules of investment, I believe that you can't go too far wrong with any investment you make, no matter what is happening in volatile financial markets. I truly believe that with these seven rules, you're never too far away from investment and financial planning success.

These seven golden rules are:

1. Never borrow to invest.

2. Keep enough cash – but not too much!!! – and find the best market cash interest rates.

3. Invest primarily to beat inflation.

4. Diversify across all five main asset classes in order to minimise investment risk and volatility.

5. Invest for the longer term and seek to involve your beneficiaries in the discussions where and when you are comfortable.

6. Find the best provider to manage your capital and to provide you with top-quality advice and service.

7. Never invest in anything you do not fully understand and do not attempt to "time" the market.

Rule number one:

Never borrow to invest

This rule is relatively straightforward: you should never borrow money to invest and you should always consider repaying debt before investing capital. Over the 18-plus years I've been working directly as a financial adviser, many clients have come to me and said something along the lines of: "I've heard your returns are very strong. I think it may be a good idea to borrow money and invest with you." My response is **always**: "I'm sorry to tell you that would be totally the wrong thing to do."

There are two main reasons for this. Firstly, when you borrow the interest rate is likely to be high and, secondly, there is no guarantee on the returns from any asset-backed, unit-linked investment. I strongly believe no investment is good enough to consider borrowing to invest in it, even if interest rates on borrowing are low and the returns on an investment appear to be high.

When you are investing, you want to keep it simple and as soon as you borrow, you're adding an unnecessary layer of complication and putting pressure on yourself and your finances because, at some point, that capital will need to be repaid. If you don't have the money to invest now, my advice to you would be to save up the money to invest, but, whatever you do, don't borrow it.

You might borrow now at a competitive interest rate, but what if interest rates go up? Or what if, in the short term at least, the investment doesn't perform as well as it needs to? All you will do is put yourself through unnecessary stress.

In addition to never borrowing to invest, I always advise my clients to consider repaying any debt they have before they invest – which includes mortgages, credit cards and personal finance, HP, PCP car loans, business loans or even loans made by friends or family – because that debt will have to be repaid at some point.

However, this is a very personal decision because there is an opportunity cost to repaying debt. Once the capital has been utilised to repay the debt, that capital, and therefore the opportunity, is lost. This is why it is a personal decision for each of my clients as to how much of their debt they repay and when they repay it. That said, I would certainly advise you to avoid high-interest borrowing as much as you can and to make sure that if you have any unsecured credit cards or personal loans, you repay those first.

Secured loans or mortgages are slightly different, especially when we are within a low interest rate environment. However, I always encourage my clients, especially those on a fixed budget, to consider a fixed interest rate where, no matter what happens to the Bank of England base interest rate, rises to their monthly repayment will not alter during the term of the fixed rate. The length of the mortgage loan term and making sure it's affordable are key. From 2004–2006, I was actively involved in helping my clients directly in the mortgage/secured loan market and I enjoyed it – I believe all financial advisers must have a strong working knowledge of this vital market for their clients. Today, I work with mortgage professionals within my firm to assist my clients on this important aspect of advice.

You may have a different view about the amount of debt you wish to hold compared to other people. As a financial adviser, it's my job to understand what level of debt you are comfortable with and how quickly you want to repay that debt before I make any recommendations. I will always encourage you to repay your debt, rather than investing, if you would like to be debt-free for your own peace of mind.

Essentially, my view is to always keep it simple, so repay any debt you have where that's possible and, for any debt you choose not to repay now, make sure you have a good repayment plan in place that perhaps has fixed rates at its core to ensure the debt is never going to take you outside of your monthly budget if interest rates go up.

Rule number two:

Keep enough cash – but not too much!!! – and find the best market cash interest rates

Cash is a terrible asset if you hold it in the long term, but it is absolutely vital for short-term liquid capital expenditure and emergencies. As a guide, I recommend that all my clients keep a minimum of at least three months' normal essential and discretionary expenditure in cash, although usually my clients hold a much larger cash reserve than this to cover all short-term (zero to five year) contingencies and any emergency needs.

The primary reason for holding enough cash (but not too much) and to invest the remainder is that WHEN financial markets experience volatility and your invested portfolio drops in value (which it will: it will go both up and down in value), then you have sufficient cash reserves for your short-term needs and contingencies. This means you do not have to rely upon or liquidate your investment portfolio. The key is to ensure you "hold your nerve" when markets fall and are not tempted to cash-in your investments.

I will highlight again the point that, should a client not be prepared to accept volatility in their portfolio, my advice is NOT to invest, but to remain in cash accounts.

To be clear, my broad guidance is to keep enough cash for your short-term needs and then to invest the remainder for a minimum five-year-plus time horizon in real assets in order to beat inflation.

At the time of writing, the UK has had a very low interest rate environment for around 20 years. These rates are likely to remain low for the foreseeable future, but with inflationary times on the horizon we may see interest rates creeping up again soon. Even if they do rise again, however, it is very unlikely that we shall return to the times we saw from the early 1980s to around 2007, when investors could hold cash accounts and still beat inflation. This is why cash is such a poor asset class to hold in large quantities: even by holding fixed-rate cash deposit bonds that have terms of three, four or five years, it is impossible to invest in cash assets long term and still beat "the devil" that is inflation. You can clearly see how this has changed over the years in the following graph.

Have your savings reached the point of no return?

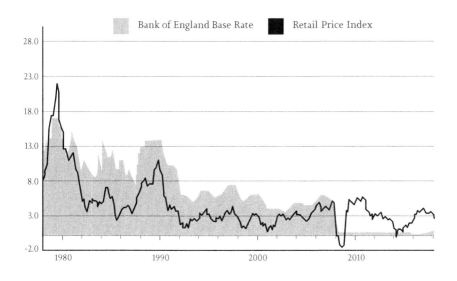

This graph highlights that, from the early 1980s to around 2007, the UK base interest rate (the shaded area) was higher than RPI (inflation – the solid line). Therefore, it is reasonable to assume that investors could have found retail cash deposit accounts from banks and building societies to beat inflation without having to invest in real assets to do so during this period. It also shows that since around 2008, inflation, despite being relatively low, has been well ahead of the UK base rate, which in December 2021 at 0.25 per cent is almost the lowest since the formation of the Bank of England in 1694. Therefore, investing in real assets has been the only client option to beat inflation since then.

"Real" returns

The issue with holding too much cash long term is that the "real" return on it (which is the return minus the effects of inflation and taxes) is terrible. Let's say that you are lucky enough to find an instant access savings account with a gross interest rate of 0.5 per cent per annum (pa). Based upon an inflation rate of, say, 3.50 per cent pa, your capital is guaranteed to lose three per cent pa. In addition, income tax must be deducted at your marginal rate (above £1000/£500 or more of annual gross interest depending upon your tax rate). The table on page 94 shows the true long-term effect of this example's three per cent drop in value of your capital.

One of the responses I'm often met with by clients who have large cash assets is: "But cash is guaranteed, Howard." Actually, it isn't. The Financial Services Compensation Scheme (FSCS) will protect us for up to £85,000 each, per individual banking licence. You might think that's fine if you spread your cash between different institutions; however, there's a potential catch. If we take an organisation like Lloyds Banking Group, they have many brands (e.g. Halifax, Bank of Scotland, Scottish Widows), but only one banking licence. That means if you have cash savings of more than £85,000 spread across different brands owned by that group, you are only covered by the FSCS guarantee up to £85,000 under their banking licence, and no more.

Therefore, if you have a large amount of cash you intend to hold, the only way to make sure it is truly guaranteed under the FSCS limits – let's be clear here and not cause unnecessary alarm (we all remember the queues outside of Northern Rock in 2008; however, depositors' cash was still made secure despite Northern Rock's problems) – in the unlikely event that an FSCS-licensed institution is unable to pay out its depositors cash, is to spread your cash between different financial institutions up to their £85,000 limits.

Let's say you have successfully managed to distribute your short-term cash reserves within FSCS protection limits. The issue then, however, becomes the uncompetitive interest rates currently being offered on cash savings accounts. This fundamentally means that, although your investment capital is guaranteed, that capital is also almost certainly guaranteed to fall backwards against inflation.

Another cash management option – and this is for cash holdings of typically £250,000 and more – is something I term a cash concierge service. There are various companies that offer this service (the one we use is Flagstone Cash Management) and they provide a secure, online and easy-to-use system which helps clients save time and hassle in having to unnecessarily open many different accounts with different providers to maintain the £85,000 per licence FSCS protections. The way these services work is that the client deposits their cash in a central "hub" bank account with one of the big four banks, and from there the client selects, via the online portal, a basket of different provider accounts which vary in hold/deposit term and all of which have been carefully selected by Flagstone or another cash concierge service.

Each deposit institution's "risk rating" is clearly high-lighted, along with the rate on offer, savings term etc and the FSCS protection afforded. The other advantage to using a cash concierge service is that they can operate at economies of scale that you, as an individual, cannot. Simply, this generally means a more competitive client interest rate, even taking their charges into account, than if a client was to seek out accounts with institutions themselves, not to mention that it is so much easier to administer.

When it comes to cash, National Savings products, such as Premium Bonds, have their place, but it's important to recognise that their longer-term hold rates are unlikely to compare favourably against inflation. That said, many of my clients enjoy the chance of the "Big One" coming in one day and hold Premium Bonds, which have a jackpot at £1 million for this very reason. In the past, National Savings have issued indexed-linked cash bonds, which are an excellent cash invest-ment and a true way to help keep your cash in pace with inflation without taking any investment risk at all.

The problem is that we have not seen any new issues of these bonds for a number of years and when they do come to market they become quickly subscribed. An advantage of working with a financial adviser who is attuned to this is that they will let you know when such rare opportunities arise – I continually keep National Savings products on my radar. The fairly recent issue of three- and five-year Pensioner Cash Bonds saw a number of clients taking them up a few years ago.

There are also peer-to-peer cash lending schemes, which can offer competitive interest rates for your cash, but it's important to note that your capital is at risk and their regulation/client protections remain at question.

Finally, I want to mention that over the years I have met a multitude of clients who were previously solely "cash investors". That is, before meeting me and taking my advice, their entire portfolio was invested in cash accounts with banks and building societies. So, after I have got to know and fully understand their aims and aspirations and after detailed conversations on how asset-backed investment funds behave, they have invested in line with the seven golden rules to good long-term effect.

Rule number three:

Invest primarily to beat inflation

Inflation is a silent killer of your money. In economics, inflation refers to general progressive increases in the prices of goods and services, so when these general price levels rise, each penny in your pound buys fewer goods and services. Essentially, inflation corresponds to a reduction in the purchasing power of money. It is currently fairly low in the UK and has been for the last 15 to 20 years, which means it often goes under our radar. That said, at the time of writing at what I hope is the tail-end of the Covid-19 pandemic, reports of higher energy prices (which will have a knock-on effect on price rises on food and consumables at the check-out) are rife. Inflation can have a seriously detrimental effect on the value of your investment capital. The following table illustrates this damaging effect of inflation clearly.

Based on a starting value of £100,000

Period Years	3% Inflation	5% Inflation
1	£97,100	£95,200
5	£86,300	£78,400
10	£74,300	£61,400
15	£64,100	£48,100
20	£55,200	£37,700

If you were around in the 1980s or the early to mid-millennium years, as I have already mentioned, you will likely remember those times when inflation and interest rates peaked. During that period, it was possible, at times, to hold bank/building society cash deposit accounts that could marginally beat inflation. However, as I explained in rule number two, this certainly isn't possible today.

Inflation essentially erodes the value of your cash because the cost of what you're buying with your money (everything from energy and food to clothes and holidays) goes up over the years, while the amount of capital you have stagnates and becomes worth less when holding cash as interest rates don't beat inflation.

Be careful of investing in "Guaranteed Structured Products"

Especially when stock markets have recently fallen, and therefore when amateur investors are fearful, a number of financial services providers often market and offer a "guaranteed" stock market-linked bond which typically will track a market index (the FTSE 100, for example) for a three- or five-year term. If an investor adds, say, £10,000 to the product then their original capital is typically guaranteed to be returned after the three- or five-year term (which you will follow is also a guarantee that their capital has fallen backwards against inflation over this period!). However, if the market index increases over the period then a percentage increase is paid to the investor. I am personally not keen on these structured products (they are invested in hedge funds and derivatives to supply the growth and guarantee potential) and here is my rationale:

- The investor pays for the guarantee (which is a guarantee to fall versus inflation as I have covered).

- The product is inflexible – it is a growth-only potential vehicle and has a fixed maturity.

- It is not well diversified.

- The growth potential is typically limited to a certain percentage upside ceiling – whereas with asset-backed funds this is not the case.

Instead, by investing in real assets across the five main asset classes that I define and explain in some depth in golden rule four, I believe the potential for longer-term, inflation-beating returns is better maximised without the investor having to pay for this guarantee. I consider these so-called "guaranteed" structured products as a "halfway house" towards investing – my view is that if you are going to invest then do so properly with top-quality fund management. My analogy is: "If you are going to go swimming then jump into the pool and swim – do not just dip your toe into the water."

This golden rule is, therefore, all about investing in real assets with the specific purpose of beating inflation. Real assets over the longer term appreciate in value and, when combined with top-quality fund management, can ensure inflation is not only hedged but also beaten. To do that effectively and to minimise investment risk, it is essential to diversify across not only the real asset classes available but also across the style and type of investment manager used, which leads us into rule number four.

Rule number four:

Diversify across all five main asset classes in order to minimise investment risk and volatility

Before I talk more about the importance of investment portfolio diversification, I'll set out and then seek to explain the five key asset classes in a little depth. This is important as, remember, in golden rule seven I ask you to "never invest in something you do not fully understand". I would argue that money, cash or capital can only be invested into these five main asset classes (although I will add a sixth asset class, which I will also cover shortly) and pretty much nowhere else so, if you do hold a diversified portfolio across all five main asset classes, you can be sure that you have a fully "hedged" and well-rounded portfolio. It is the skill of the financial adviser to ensure that you understand each asset class and that your portfolio is structured such that you will achieve the longer-term targeted income and growth returns your appetite for investment risk allows.

My five main asset classes are:

1. Cash and cash accounts (enough for the short term only remember!)

2. Fixed interest (government and/or corporate bonds)

3. Shares (also known as equities)

4. Commodity assets (gold, silver, minerals, copper, wheat etc)

5. Residential and commercial property (I include infrastructure within this asset class too)

The sixth asset class is investments usually owned personally and bought for pleasure of ownership as well as investment potential. Here I include articles such as artwork, paintings, race horses and classic cars, and I would place miscellaneous investments in here too, such as Bitcoin and Cryptocurrency.

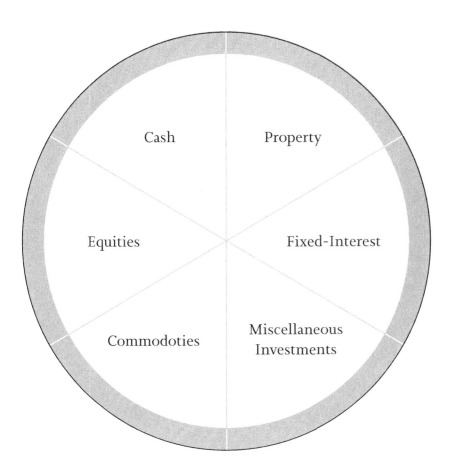

Cash Property

Equities Fixed-Interest

Commodoties Miscellaneous Investments

To some of you reading this, diversifying your investments across the different asset classes might seem like
common sense; to others this might be a completely new
concept and your current investments may be centred
in only one or two of the six asset classes already
described. This could well have happened by default
rather than due to a conscious decision to specifically

target these investment areas – for example, you may now have all of your money in cash accounts and own a residential property (two asset classes). However, do you realise that by owning a simple employer DC pension plan, you are also very likely to be invested in fixed interest, equity and perhaps even commercial property as well as the commodity asset classes just mentioned? So, without perhaps realising it, you are already a diversified, long-term investor across all the main asset classes.

One of my long-standing clients, who is a farmer in Yorkshire, once said to me many years ago: "Is money then like muck, Howard? You have to spread the muck about to get the crops to grow the best?" This is what I'd like you to bear in mind when you're looking at overall investment diversification – spread the "muck" about and therefore spread your investment risk.

There are two parts to diversification that you should consider. The first is to diversify across asset classes, and the second is to diversify across different asset class fund managers who have different styles of investing. This may involve investing in both active and passive funds to provide a further broad diversification. The following table shows why it is so important to diversify your investments across the main asset classes I have set out – you can see that no one asset class has consistently performed the best, year in, year out; however, the diversified portfolio, invested across all asset classes, hedges investment risk. Remember, all we want to do is, as securely as possible, beat inflation.

2016	2017	2018	2019	2020
US Equities 34%	Emerging Markets Equity 25%	UK Gilts 1%	US Equities 31%	Emerging Markets Equity 25%
Commodities 33%	Far East Equities 19%	Deposit A/c 1%	Emerging Markets Equity 25%	US Equities 14%
Emerging Markets Equity 25%	European Equities 15%	US Equities 1%	European Equities 19%	Far East Equities 14%
Far East Equities 28%	UK Equities 13%	Commodities -6%	UK Equities 19%	Deposit A/c 0%
European Equities 21%	US Equities 11%	Far East Equities -8%	Far East Equities 19%	European Equities 0%
UK Equities 17%	UK Gilts 2%	European Equities -9%	Commodities 8%	UK Gilts 6%
UK Gilts 10%	Deposit A/c 0%	UK Equities -10%	UK Gilts 7%	Commodities -6%
Deposit A/c 1%	Commodities -7%	Emerging Markets Equity 25%	Deposit A/c 1%	UK Equities -12%

I've already talked about cash as an asset class, how vital it is for all clients to hold sufficient cash for their short-term needs and some of the potential pitfalls associated with holding it for too long. Now I'd like to explore and define some of the other asset classes I've described in a little more detail, as hopefully from the table you can see the diversification benefits of holding all the main asset classes longer term.

Fixed-interest assets

Government gilts

The term "gilt-edged" comes from the fact that loans (or stock) issued and therefore backed by the UK government (or typically any other overseas government, but bear in mind that some countries' debt is more risky than others!) are very secure – the UK government has never defaulted on these loans/stock. However, while they are very secure that doesn't mean they are always a desirable investment. The following example shows how the value of government gilts can fluctuate.

In 1932, the then-Chancellor of the Exchequer Neville Chamberlain issued a government-backed 3.5 per cent undated War Loan Stock[2]. This War Loan Stock, quite simply, would pay out a fixed and guaranteed annual interest rate (typically referred to as a "coupon") of

2 HM Treasury and The Rt Hon George Osborne, (2014), 'Chancellor to repay the nation's First World War debt', Gov.uk, 3 December, available at: https://www.gov.uk/government/news/chancellor-to-repay-the-nations-first-world-war-debt

3.5 per cent – a great deal for the client when interest rates are low, such as at the time of writing at the end of 2021 when the Bank of England base rate is just 0.25 per cent[3]. However, it was much less attractive in October 1989, for example, when the base rate was a staggering 14.88 per cent.

In basic terms, this means if you owned £100 of a 3.5 per cent War Loan Stock, it would pay 3.5 per cent interest/coupon every year. On the face of it, that's an attractive, government-backed holding paying (in this example) a secure annual interest rate of 3.5 per cent.

However, what do you think happened to the price of this £100 of War Loan Stock in October 1989 when the base rate was 14.88 per cent? You would be right if you said that the price dropped much lower than £100. The reason for this was that the War Loan Stock was paying only a fixed 3.5 per cent rate, whereas market bank/building society rates would typically have been in excess of the 14.88 per cent base rate. Therefore, the War Loan Stock was not as attractive to hold, as much higher market cash savings rates were available.

3 Bank of England, (2021), 'Bank Rate increased to 0.25% – December 2021', 16 December, available at: https://www.bankofengland.co.uk/monetary-policy-summary-and-minutes/2021/december-2021

We need to remember that, no matter how secure the gilt-edged stock is, it is traded on a gilt market and therefore, in a similar way to stock markets, the price of the gilt will fluctuate on a daily basis as will the price of the underlying gilt fund. When interest rates go up, the price of a gilt like the War Loan Stock is likely to go down (as it is less attractive to hold) and when interest rates go down the reverse is true.

So, even though the 3.5 per cent War Loan Stock was a secure, UK government-backed investment, offering a competitive (certainly in today's terms) interest rate, both the gilt and therefore the underlying unit trust (if it was held/selected by the gilt fund manager) would fluctuate in value and in some cases, especially when interest rates moved sharply, could be even more volatile than an equity/share fund.

Corporate bonds

Another fixed-interest option, slightly different to gilts, is corporate bonds. These are issued typically by large corporate firms and, similar to gilts, will offer a fixed coupon/interest rate and a redemption date. The size of the interest rate offered is dictated often by the strength of the issuing company (a AAA-rated firm will offer a lower rate typically than a BBB-rated firm due to the risk associated with redemption/repayment of the debt) and the timeframe length of the bond to redemption. As part of a diversified investment portfolio, corporate bonds as well as gilts have a part to play within the fixed-interest asset class. UK gilts are very securely backed and there has never been a default. However, there is a greater default repayment risk on corporate bonds, so it will follow that the rate offered on them is generally less attractive than that offered on a gilt. In addition, the higher the "investment grade" of the corporate bond, the less attractive the underlying rate that is offered.

I would recommend that, as part of a diversified portfolio, rather than trying to choose gilts and/or corporate bonds yourself, you instead tap into the expertise of an experienced fixed-rate fund manager who will typically diversify across a wide selection and number of gilt/corporate bond holdings with different terms and risk profiles. They will also professionally and carefully manage the fund to avoid volatility and be attuned to market-related factors and interest rate movements that could affect your returns.

Another point to bear in mind on diversification is that investing narrowly and exclusively in fixed-interest stock, and therefore more cautious funds, won't necessarily protect your capital from sharp market fluctuations. I have experienced this first-hand when working at NatWest in and around 2001. Gartmore (who were at that time the bank's only appointed external fund manager) launched what proved to be a very popular, strongly performing, fixed-interest fund. Clients were keen to invest in it because it was perceived to be very low risk. However, when interest rates moved sharply upwards, the price dropped dramatically. Any clients who had solely invested in that fund (and therefore not followed the asset class diversification rule) suffered sharp short-term losses despite the "cautious" nature of the fixed-interest fund. Those clients who were diversified, however, and held the other asset class funds saw their portfolio continue to beat inflation as their risk was "hedged" and therefore offset.

I am sometimes asked the question: "Why is a fixed-interest fund seen as more cautious than an equity/share fund?" The answer is simply that in the event of a company liquidation, the corporate bond (or debenture bond) holders are paid out before the share/

equity holders, which means the risk for corporate bondholders is lower.

Residential property

Many clients tell me that they like and feel secure by investing in residential property and often this is because it is an asset they can see and, of course, understand (which fulfils my requirement under the seventh golden rule). They like the fact that it is "tangible" and they enjoy physically owning this asset (and seeing/visiting/refurbishing it if it is owned locally and close to their own home). Ownership through a Land Registry "title deed" also gives them comfort.

However, once I have explained, and my client thoroughly understands, the other asset classes covered here (which, remember, are also real and tangible) they will often realise that, by holding too much residential property, not only will their portfolio lack diversification but also there will be similar investment risk and volatility issues by owning property directly, as well as additional ownership and taxation pitfalls.

If you own a main residence that's worth perhaps £100,000 or considerably more, you are already heavily invested in the residential property asset class. Buying more residential property to rent out in the hope of a strong income yield and/or longer-term capital appreciation can lead to a loss of asset class diversification and also expose you to a number of additional risks.

So, what are these additional property ownership risks?

Taxation risk:
Rental income is taxable at your marginal income tax rate. Outside of your main residence ownership, on sale/disposal any gain in value is subject to capital gains tax (CGT). Does the client complete the HMRC tax account/return themselves (time taken) or employ a local accountant (cost)? Is there any stamp duty payable when you buy it?

Tenant management risk:
Quite rightly, a tenant's safety and residing rights need to be fully secured and their contract properly documented with an owner's responsibility to keep on top of fast-changing and ever-increasing safety/property management legislation. Does the owner tackle this management themselves or employ a professional

letting agent? Either option comes with the associated ownership time and/or cost burdens.

Void period risk:

What happens when the paying tenant moves out? How is a new tenant sourced and both their ability to pay the required rent and to look after the property demonstrated? What is the frequency of property condition progress checks, who undertakes these checks and is the tenant contractually obliged to allow property access to enable them to be undertaken?

Market risk:

We are all aware of the term "negative equity"; property prices will fall and rise in accordance with local market supply and demand. The owner/investor takes on this risk themselves and there is no guarantee that property prices will always rise. That said, a client with strong local property market knowledge can, of course, find a bargain, but the reverse is equally true and I have seen a number of clients over the years holding properties which have current sale values far less than their original purchase prices. Also, does a chartered surveyor need to assess the property condition etc and at what cost?

Liquidity risk:

Property takes time to sell. In a difficult market and with a property in the wrong location how long will it take? A conveyancing solicitor must be hired (on both the purchase, where thorough due diligence at the outset is required on property rights/easements/boundaries/local searches etc, and on the ultimate sale) with the associated cost incurred.

Property maintenance risk:

What happens when, as is inevitable, a new roof, ridge tile or gas boiler is needed or what if rising damp begins? The potential maintenance list is endless and the costs incurred eat into the underlying rental yield. Will the property owner, who does not use a professional letting agent (who will usually field the tenant calls for help), also be prepared for the late-night call to fix the tenant's leaking bath or shower while enjoying their Saturday night takeaway? Remember, it is all the owner's ultimate responsibility.

Time risk:

Do you have the time to undertake these responsibilities? Are you "handy" at property maintenance yourself and would you enjoy maintaining the property throughout your period of ownership?

Borrowing/gearing risk:

Are you buying the property outright or is a mortgage required? The latter will usually require the services (and charges) of a professional mortgage broker who will seek to find the best "buy-to-let" mortgage deal according to your circumstances. We then have the interest rate risk: do you fix the outset interest rate and for what term to protect against potential rate rises? Is the mortgage loan repayable on an "interest-only" basis (meaning the loan amount will not reduce over the mortgage term) and, if so, how is the loan ultimately to be repaid? How much deposit is being paid? This is important as we then consider "gearing", which is the ratio of property equity to debt. It is important for the amateur landlord to remember that the mortgage lender takes a legal property title charge and can seek a deadline repayment schedule of the loan. This forces the mortgage owner to either remortgage to new lenders or liquidate their property on a forced-sale basis to repay the loan. This has happened to a couple of my clients who were "highly geared". I can vividly recall the stress of my client as they wrestled under time pressures to make the new remortgage deals, which was not a great experience for them, but happily they did manage to remortgage.

Clearly, I have not painted a particularly pretty picture of residential property investment. However, I do believe that as part of a larger and well-diversified overall client investment portfolio residential property has a part to play, as long as it has been carefully considered and the underlying properties judiciously selected (location, location, location etc). However, my clear warning is to understand the risks fully before investing and have a clear plan on the income yield sought and how it will be derived, as well as the required and anticipated longer-term capital appreciation targeted.

In discussing and highlighting the benefits of professional fund management, I need to point out that an investor cannot typically invest into a residential property fund as they are extremely limited in availability.

Commercial property

The definition of this asset class is fairly straightforward: commercial property is property owned and used for a business or commercial purpose. It includes shops, offices, factories, car showrooms and many other business premises.

I have highlighted a number of pitfalls and some advantages of owning residential property and many of these equally apply to direct ownership of commercial property so I will not repeat them here.

Most investors will see the benefit of holding commercial property as an asset class as part of a diversified portfolio but, unlike residential property ownership, most people will not have direct exposure to it. A commercial property fund, however, will afford you as an investor this opportunity without the worry of complete and outright property ownership.

A good commercial property fund manager will pool their investors' capital and invest in good-quality commercial property for two major upsides, similar to residential buy-to-let investments, namely, income yield (rentals) and capital appreciation.

The skill and expertise of the commercial property fund manager is absolutely critical here. You are looking for carefully and competitively acquired, sought-after commercial property acquisitions in prime business locations where the business occupiers are brought in on long and upwardly repairing (increasing rentals) leases. Those fund managers who can spot buying opportunities and see longer-term market potential will clearly thrive. My question to an amateur investor in any commercial property fund is how do you know whether your appointed fund manager has the necessary expertise and also are they being regularly fed "new money" so that they can make new and judiciously considered acquisitions with your hard-earned cash? Again, this is where the advice of a financial adviser can be invaluable.

Investing in infrastructure through a professional fund manager is also worthy of consideration as part of a fully diversified investment portfolio. An infrastructure fund invests in companies providing water and sewer services, utilities, shipping and waste management, and oil and gas pipelines, amongst other public services that people rely upon to live. The key here is that a "small investment is beautiful", as infrastructure funds are highly illiquid but again can decrease volatility as part of a balanced portfolio.

Shares/equities

The fourth of the five asset classes and, certainly for long-term growth, perhaps the most vital and probably most volatile of the asset classes is share or equity ownership. Earlier in the book they are placed at the apex of my "pyramid of risk" – they are the riskiest and most volatile asset class to hold, but they also come with the best upside growth potential.

In the UK owning an "ordinary share" (also known as an equity) gives the holder entitlement to voting rights at annual meetings, as well as an entitlement to a dividend income payment (should the company make a profit – these are usually paid on an annual basis). The shareholder therefore has part ownership of the underlying either private or public limited company. Private limited company shares are not traded on a recognised public stock market (as the name suggests, they are owned privately), so it is public limited company shares that are often acquired by private investors or professional fund managers as they can be bought and sold easily.

A success story and a cautionary tale of share ownership

Back in the 1980s under Margaret Thatcher's government, many of the then-government-owned public corporations such as BT, British Gas and British Airways were sold ("privatised") on the UK stock market as public limited companies, making share ownership both available and therefore popular to the small investor. When, in 1986, the Conservative government urged investors to snap up shares in British Gas, around four million people bought the shares at their offer price of 135p, with many selling them (including myself as a young bank clerk at the time) back on the stock market for a quick profit. Had I held onto them, instead of selling my British Gas shares (now BG Group) so quickly for my "fast buck", not only would I have seen the price rise to a whopping 1034.50p today (28 February 2022), but I would also have enjoyed an annual dividend payment along the way.

Here comes the share ownership lesson, however. Just as British Gas has been a small shareholders' success story, the privatisation of Railtrack in 1994 was a disaster. Renamed RT Group plc in 2002, it was dissolved on 22 June 2010 and all the shareholders, of course, lost their invested cash.

Shares are inherently riskier than fixed-interest corporate bonds because, as mentioned previously, in the event of a company liquidation, they are last to be paid out. This is one reason why they are more volatile. They do, however, attach real asset company ownership and allow the investor to enjoy the upside growth potential and dividend distributions when profits are strong. Shares are where the investor will benefit from longer-term, inflation-beating returns, but be prepared for the volatility associated with stock market peaks and troughs.

Here is where I need to explain the difference between investment speculation (or gambling) and careful, judicious, professional fund management investing.

I can recall a number of clients over the years who have bought shares, usually via a self-selected online platform using their own judgement or after getting a "tip from a mate down the pub". Sometimes I have met clients with up to £100,000 and more invested using their own judgement, maybe spread across only a handful of shareholdings. Even more frequently, I see clients who are working for a major PLC and have acquired bonus payment shareholdings and share options/ stock options in that one company, again typically valued at tens of thousands of pounds. I always then explain my very own hard luck story.

Howard's story

I worked for NatWest Bank from 1982–2004 and each year I would diligently take any annual bonus in shares (instead of cash) and also pay into their sharesave scheme from my salary. Year after year, the NatWest share price kept going upwards and I would congratulate myself on the successful investment decisions I was making each year. In early 2000, NatWest was taken over by the Royal Bank of Scotland, but still the share price kept rolling ever upwards UNTIL disaster struck.

During the financial crisis of 2008, the Royal Bank of Scotland (then renamed RBS) was one of the banks bailed out by the UK government, receiving public funds to the effect of £45.5 billion. In January 2007, the RBS share price was 10225.20p, but due to the bailout it fell to just 220p by January 2009. I had tens of thousands of pounds invested in RBS. Had I practised what I preach and sold this one share at regular intervals across the years, diversifying into the five main asset classes and using professional fund managers then, instead of nursing huge losses, my investments would have comfortably beaten inflation. Holding one single company share, no matter how strong you perceive it to be, comes with the associated risk that you could be holding another RBS share or, perhaps an even worse example, a Northern Rock share which, of course, was valued at its peak in 2006 at over £12.00 but then, following its collapse on 12 October 2012, (just like Railtrack) became completely worthless!

My point here is simple: buying shares yourself is merely gambling or, at best, speculation and you must understand your risk. Do you enjoy the thrill of speculating on shares? If so, use only a small investment amount (that you can afford to lose) or why not join a local "share club" who will often meet monthly, pick a few shares socially and enjoy the profit or loss associated without having a major financial amount at stake.

Those clients who do own a large portfolio of shares (and therefore a large overall investment portfolio – I would a define "large" portfolio as a minimum of £500,000 invested in unit-linked funds excluding pensions) may benefit from professional fund management of those shares or a new direct investment addition to a share portfolio, for a number of reasons. Using a Discretionary Fund Manager (DFM), a firm whose expertise is managing individual shares directly, affords the client some major advantages.

The following is a brief list of the advantages of a DFM solution:

- "In specie" transfer (a direct transfer – no sale made) of the client's existing directly held shares to the DFM provider (avoids any immediate taxation issues as the transferred shares are not sold).

- Management of the client's ISA and CGT positions on an ongoing annual basis.

- Provision of tax-efficient income streams should the client require this.

- "Selling down" of the client's existing direct shareholdings to diversify investment risk into unitised funds and different asset classes should the client want to have an even lower risk position with the portfolio in time.

Shares are a riskier asset class; however, by using a professional fund manager who will diversify across perhaps over 100 (or more) different shares, the risk is reduced to avoid an RBS, Railtrack or Northern Rock loss scenario. I have focused on the UK share market and UK share funds here; however, it is important to mention that international and global share funds also have a key part to play in a fully diversified share portfolio. "Niche" international funds perhaps involved in one country only (e.g. "China Special Opportunities" or "Emerging Market" funds) are usually inherently more volatile than more general UK or European funds and it requires the skill of the financial adviser to point out this potential risk/reward and to ensure a client is content to accept the additional risk associated with them.

Alternative assets (Commodities)

Funds investing in alternative assets such as gold, silver, minerals, wheat, corn and other commodities offer further balance and spread to a portfolio. Often, when share markets have taken a tumble downwards we see the popular press and the national news mentioning that there has been a "flight to gold" and that "gold is the asset class to buy as you can see it and rely on it". Before we all go out and buy our gold bars (and over the years I have seen clients do just this, especially when share markets have been difficult), let's remember that gold is only one alternative asset. It is traded on a market, so will be volatile and, while it can form a key piece of a diversified portfolio, it is important not to put all of our capital into it.

Alternative assets can be owned through a professional fund manager (often called "multi-asset funds") and, when held with a combination of the other asset classes, can be a good way to de-risk a spread portfolio. I will talk about some other miscellaneous asset investment options in Chapter 7, which I have called my sixth asset class.

Diversification doesn't only apply to assets – diversify your fund managers too

As part of a balanced portfolio, it is important to consider diversifying your portfolio across different fund managers with differing styles and strategies, especially with share funds. You now understand both the definition of a fund manager and the advantages of professional fund management, as well as asset class diversification, so it will make sense to consider diversification in this sense too.

There are many different styles and strategies and I would like to briefly outline what I consider to be the main four relating to share investing:

Value investing:

Value fund managers typically aim to acquire "unloved" or "out of favour" companies at a cheap price then hold them longer term to achieve capital appreciation. At the core of value investing is the belief that all shares have an intrinsic value defined by mathematical analysis. An example might be if a share's intrinsic value is £10 per share it would only be bought by the fund manager if its price was, say, £7.50 or below, and it would be sold once the market price returns to the intrinsic or fair value of £10 for a healthy profit.

Growth investing:

This strategy focuses on finding businesses that have the greatest potential to expand in both size and importance within their market sectors. Whereas value investing is about the intrinsic value and numbers, a flaw of the value style is that growth company share opportunities can be missed. For example, since the global financial crisis of 2008, much of the stock market rally has been driven by growth rather than value shares – the FAANG group. The main characteristics of a growth fund manager style are high-potential growth rates rather than high-dividend returns, as often high-growth companies funnel their earnings by reinvesting to fuel this growth.

Quality investing:

This style is based upon an enduringly simple principle – that quality businesses have a greater likelihood of delivering quality returns in both good and bad economic times. The concept of "quality" first entered the investment world in the fixed-interest markets, where bonds were evaluated by specialist ratings firms such as Moody's and Standard and Poor's. This is applied by quality investing share fund managers who seek to buy quality companies at a good value price in the belief that a quality share will not only provide strong growth but also return profits to inves-tors through a good dividend yield.

Momentum investing:

Essentially momentum investing is based on the concept of selling losers and buying winners. In reality, momentum investing looks to take advantage of market volatility by taking short-term positions on shares that are rising and then exiting those positions as soon as the shares look to have peaked, i.e. when they lose "momentum". I gave an example of momentum investing earlier in the book when I mentioned the Rolls Royce share price fluctuation in 2021 – a low of 87p to a high of £1.50 all within the space of a year – a buy low/sell high here would have rewarded the investor or fund manager handsomely.

Clearly then it is important to have different styles of fund manager to take advantage of the various invest-ment strategies available, particularly in the share asset class. I would also suggest that a well-diversified share asset class holding has both active fund manage-ment and an element of passive fund management (as defined earlier in the book) to give even wider diversity.

As a general rule, I recommend that my clients invest in a portfolio of a minimum and an outline maximum of between eight and 12 different funds, diversifying across asset classes, as well as style and type of fund manager.

For clients investing larger amounts, perhaps £500,000 and more, as covered above, I may suggest even wider diversification using a DFM portfolio, investing both directly and indirectly (the latter via funds) in shares and also, depending upon their taxation position, using Venture Capital Trusts (VCTs) and Enterprise Investment Schemes (EIS). Those clients who already own a property portfolio will usually be advised to retain it provided they are comfortable with the risks I have highlighted in regard to property ownership because, in a large client portfolio, property ownership can provide much-needed diversification.

Before any client recommendation is put forward, as I explained in Chapter 1, it is essential I understand my client's clear long-term objective and my client must confirm to me their complete understanding of the associated product risks before we move ahead with a recommendation.

I hope within this section on investment diversification that I have thoroughly highlighted a key message that, in order to formulate a well-rounded, longer-term investment portfolio, you consider investing widely. Or, if you do choose instead to focus more narrowly on only one (for example, property) or two asset classes then you at least need to be comfortable with the increased risk this narrower focus extends.

The skill of the diligent financial adviser is to match your diversification requirements both in terms of your asset class investment understanding and its application into your investment portfolio. Are your circumstances more complex or simplistic? If they are the latter, you may want to do it all yourself. If the former, then forging a relationship with a financial planner who you know, like and trust could be a sound long-term decision. This important diversification rule leads nicely into my fifth rule.

Rule number five:

Invest for the longer term and seek to involve your beneficiaries in the discussions where and when you are comfortable

There is an addition to this: invest for the long term, but keep your income options open. Many of my clients invest capital immediately to take an income (often when they have retired) and need their underlying capital to continue to grow and to beat inflation. When I say long term, I mean a minimum of five years, the simple reason being that none of us can predict the short-term nature of the markets. You have to give your appointed fund managers time to achieve growth.

Or to give you a gardening analogy, it's important to plant the seed potatoes and allow them time to grow.

In my opinion, a client should not invest any capital into the five asset classes covered earlier via fund management – or indeed any type of market-related investment designed to beat inflation – unless they have a minimum investment timeframe of five years or more. I will go even further to say that I won't accept client investment money should a client have a shorter timeframe than five years. Instead I would advise them to hold cash via perhaps fixed-rate cash bonds or National Savings. So, five years is the very minimum timeframe to invest; however, of course, the longer the better.

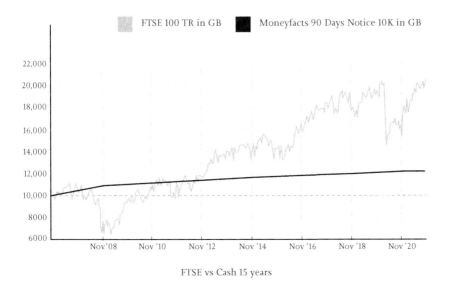

FTSE vs Cash 15 years

This graph shows the relative performance of £10,000 invested in the FTSE 100, versus Moneyfacts' 90 day notice cash accounts over a 16-year period between 2006 and 2021. The FTSE over this period achieved a 100 per cent-plus return with the net £10,000 returning over £20,500, whereas the cash accounts improved to only £12,205.26. This demonstrates the benefits of longer-term passive equity investment rather than holding cash (source FE Analytics).

As we all know, there can be difficult times, difficult days and even full-scale crashes in financial markets and, in the short term, these can affect the value of investments, but history tells us that markets bounce back given sufficient time – just look at the previous graph and the one that follows. This is why it is vital to keep enough money in cash (golden rule number two) so that when we experience market turbulence we stay fully invested.

Problems can arise if a client panics when markets fall sharply (for example, in February 2020 due to the Covid-19 pandemic) where the temptation is to turn a portfolio to cash funds in the hope of limiting downside losses. The client who does come out of invested assets for the safety of cash then faces a difficult dilemma: when do I go back into my investment portfolio?

Often, in my experience, this is when markets have settled and then recovered. Unfortunately for the client now invested in cash assets, they have missed these often particularly strong days of market growth. The vast majority of my clients, however, stay fully invested because we have ensured they have sufficient cash for the short term and plenty of income for their day-to-day needs.

Investment markets do not like uncertainty and that is why they can be so volatile. Even seasoned and experienced investors can find it difficult to hold their nerve and to stay fully invested through times like the Covid-19 pandemic, the global financial crisis in 2007/2008, 9/11, the dot-com bubble burst in 2001 and Black Monday in 1987. Amidst these times I have often had clients say to me: "It's different this time though, Howard". So far in my 39-year financial career it hasn't been and, given sufficient time, markets have recovered as have my clients' investment portfolios.

This time it's different...

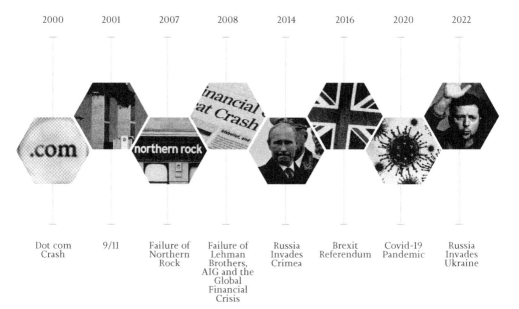

2000	2001	2007	2008	2014	2016	2020	2022
Dot com Crash	9/11	Failure of Northern Rock	Failure of Lehman Brothers, AIG and the Global Financial Crisis	Russia Invades Crimea	Brexit Referendum	Covid-19 Pandemic	Russia Invades Ukraine

This is why it is so vital for the financial adviser to take time with a client to explain and to fully check their understanding of their appetite for investment volatility and risk, as it is an absolute given that fund management or real asset market investment will have swings both up and down. I might need two, three or even four or more meetings with a client before I can see that they understand how their investments will move, and it's especially vital for me to take the time to educate those clients who have never invested before in real fund assets. I much prefer a client to stay invested in cash (in fact, I will not accept their investment capital) where I cannot see that, firstly, they fully understand how investments can, and will, move and, secondly, that they will be comfortable longer term with the explanations given.

This is why golden rule number two (keep enough cash) is so important because it allows you to ride out the inevitable ups and downs in markets without the pressure to liquidate investments.

Of course, when you reach the retirement or decumulation stage of life, where you are relying upon taking income from your pensions and investments, a financial adviser should consider what is known as sequencing or longevity risk. Without going into too much detail here, sequencing risk protection is recommending that clients invest in carefully tailored "income in retirement" portfolios specifically designed to protect their investments, both when they are taking an income and when financial markets are experiencing downturns.

Longevity risk is ensuring that upon retiring, a client will – when taking all of their current pensions, investments, cash and other assets – have enough income to last them for the remainder of their life, given their projected expenditure requirements.

In addition, involving your beneficiaries in any investment decisions should always be considered by your financial adviser and this becomes particularly important as you get older when the next generation is getting closer to benefitting and your capacity to understand investment complexity is perhaps diminishing. This is a very personal choice and the timing of any family meeting must be carefully planned and prepared by the adviser, who knows their client and the family well. Intergenerational planning (pass it on) is within the book's title and I cannot stress enough the importance of and benefits gained by involving your financial beneficiaries in your long-term financial plan.

These points lead nicely onto rule six – finding both the best fund managers for your investments and the best financial adviser firm or wealth management company for your requirements.

Rule number six:

Find the best provider to manage your capital and to provide you with top-quality advice and service

Defining the "best" provider is, of course, completely subjective. Financial advice is very much a "people" business, and the strength of the relationship you forge with your financial adviser, as I have covered already, is paramount.

Why do I think that your relationship is more important than the advisory firm you choose? I'll start with the basics. The vast majority of financial services advisory firms who provide face-to-face financial advice in the UK are regulated by the Financial Conduct Authority (FCA); therefore, choosing an FCA-regulated firm is a minimum standard choice.

FCA regulation demonstrates that a firm is governed and regulated and that they must adhere to detailed FCA rules and guidelines. These afford the client important security advantages, such as treating clients fairly (TCF) policy adherence, transparency of charges/fees and their fit and proper governance standards, amongst other valuable client protections.

Happily then, FCA-regulated firms can be relied upon for their honesty, integrity and reputation, and clients have a further back-up protection offered by the Financial Ombudsman Service (FOS).

In addition, the financial advisers representing these firms must pass, as a minimum requirement in the UK, a level four-equivalent technical qualification which the Chartered Insurance Institute term the "Regulated Diploma". This has to happen before they are authorised to provide regulated financial advice to clients, as well as passing "firm-specific" internal knowledge and skill checks to reach "competent adviser status". Once the adviser has achieved "competent adviser status", they will then follow an annual continuing professional development (CPD) programme tailored to their learning needs and the markets they operate in.

Just as you will go to see your chartered accountant to complete your complex tax return or you will see a chartered physiotherapist to solve your back or neck problem, in a similar way, today the top financial advisory firms may offer you an adviser who has achieved the title of chartered financial planner (a level six-equivalent qualification), having met the in-depth qualification and experience levels demanded by the Chartered Insurance Institute.

I was delighted to see that the financial advisory industry introduced this higher qualification standard and I wear my chartered "badge", which I obtained almost ten years ago, with pride. The study undertaken has helped me enormously with my client advice and recommendation preparation, especially in the areas where client needs become more complex, such as inheritance tax mitigation advice. I think our industry, in a similar way to accountancy, should have the chartered qualification as its minimum standard and certainly there is talk of this happening in the medium term.

When you are looking for a financial adviser, I would suggest that you seek out one who is chartered, or certainly well on their way to becoming chartered, for two main reasons. Firstly, achieving chartered status takes dedication and someone who has gone that extra mile has demonstrated a commitment to their profession and so, indirectly, their commitment to looking after their clients. Secondly, becoming chartered demonstrates the adviser's commitment to continued learning. As I'm sure you're aware, the financial services industry is always evolving, and you want an adviser who is prepared to evolve with it and stay at the forefront of the latest changes.

The next thing to understand is that there are two main types of financial advisory firms in the UK: independent financial advisers (IFAs) and restricted advisers (RAs). IFAs can, in theory, choose client products on a totally unbiased basis, freely and independently from the "whole" market. As a result, they will typically market themselves as being able to access any fund, product provider, investment or pension vehicle, or provider platform available.

Contrast this with the RA firm who are limited in their product choice to those products that have been appointed and chosen to sit solely on their own "panel". Therefore, in theory, their choice of product becomes somewhat limited.

However, in my experience the IFA firm will largely use very similar products and services to the RA firm. Typically, the IFA firm will appoint a "platform" product provider and it is from that platform that the IFA chooses their products, in a similar way to the RA adviser choosing products from their "panel". I would go on to argue that the RA firm, having carefully chosen products and services from the whole market and then added those providers to their "panel", has completed even more due diligence than the IFA firm who have simply chosen their platform provider.

So, overriding this IFA or RA polarisation choice, my firm view is that the financial adviser relationship across my three key elements of service, advice and performance together with the qualification standard your appointed financial adviser has achieved (or shows demonstrable progress towards achieving), is more important than the polarisation (IFA or RA) of the firm.

Once you have chosen your financial adviser and the underlying appointed firm for service and advice, let's now focus on how you seek to choose and appoint your fund managers and compare and contrast how an IFA broadly does this versus an example of how the RA firm I have been with for the last 18 years does it.

I explained in the first chapter how fund management works and what a fund manager is and does. Understanding this is crucial when it comes to choosing the best provider to manage your capital. The company I have been proud to represent since 2004 is a restricted advice (RA) firm. I am now going to explain why I believe the firm I represent is in a unique position when it comes to managing client funds. Using their economies of scale they are in a very strong position, as they adopt a carefully constructed mechanism to select, monitor and then change (where and when appropriate) their externally appointed fund managers.

Using their economies of scale, they appoint leading investment consultants who report to an investment committee. The role of these consultants is to scour the globe to find and recommend to the committee the very best fund managers available in each asset class. Appointed fund managers are then held to account for their performance via an open-ended contract, giving the firm the ability to terminate the relationship and substitute another carefully chosen manager should they deem it necessary.

However, fund managers are appointed for the longer term and the right to remove a manager is an added protection used only when a manager moves away from their outset mandate. In choosing fund managers, they typically do not seek to follow the latest investment fad or fashion, nor do they rely upon last year's top-performing fund data (which can often mean the following

12 months are not so good). Instead they prefer to identify and get to know individually talented fund managers who they want to work with over the long term.

This process of thorough due diligence results in solid and trusted relationships with their appointed fund managers, who are keen to have a contract with the firm I represent as this gives them access to a steady stream of new investment money to work with. Equally, and again due to the size of the funds under management and the economies of scale this affords, my firm can appoint top-quality managers on carefully negotiated fee structures, which then gives the client a pricing advantage.

With regards to diversification, they have a wide variety of fund managers across all asset classes, with differing styles and strategies. I like to adopt a portfolio approach when recommending any client investment or pension proposal, and the firm I represent has carefully tailored and diversified portfolios which match my client's chosen appetite for volatility and risk, covering my golden rule number four on diversification perfectly well.

Should my client prefer a bespoke fund selection, I can help construct something suitable with their agreement and, where necessary, I can call upon their head office management team of asset management specialists for help and advice. Should I require it, I can recommend to my clients further investment diversification via a Discretionary Fund Manager (DFM) as covered previously.

Therefore, from an investment and fund management perspective, this approach provides me with the reassurance that I, as a chartered financial planner, can get on with my important day job of providing holistic advice and service to my clients, safe in the knowledge I can rely upon the firm's expertise and experience on the vital fund management side of things.

Contrast this approach with that of an IFA. As well as providing holistic financial planning and service to their clients, the IFA also has full responsibility for the selection, monitoring and changing of funds, whereas for an adviser at the RA firm I represent this is fully taken care of in the background as I've explained. This is a tough task for the IFA: providing both holistic client advice and service and ensuring top investment fund management performance. Imagine this IFA having a client bank of 200-plus clients – I would argue they have double the workload of an adviser at my firm and, really, how can a high-street IFA compete with the detailed and judicious investment approach taken by my firm? Quite simply, in my view, they cannot.

Contrast this again with a client who chooses not to work with a financial adviser and therefore is responsible for their own financial advice, product provider service and their portfolio performance monitoring. This really is a big task to get completely right, especially when the client has complex financial circumstances.

Can you see how the three elements I talked about in the last chapter all tie together here? What I'm talking about is having strong performance of your portfolio, with holistic advice that is tailored to your circumstances and an ongoing service that ensures the products you have invested in remain suitable throughout your life and succeed to your next generation.

This is why the choice of investment firm is so important. If you are considering using an IFA, ask about their process for the continuous selection, monitoring and changing of their appointed fund managers; find out who will take care of that, how often it will happen and what research will have been carried out to support their decisions around any changes they make. As I said at the beginning of this section, the vast majority of IFA and/or restricted firm providers, so long as they are FCA regulated, will be reputable, but can they continually deliver on all three of my measures of service, advice and performance?

Rule number seven:

Never invest in anything you do not fully understand and do not try to "time" the market

It's not uncommon that a client will phone me to tell me about an investment opportunity they have been offered and to ask for my opinion. The conversation might go a little something like this: "Hi, Howard, I've been offered an opportunity with a guaranteed 12 per cent return and no risk to capital with XYZ provider, what do you think?" OR – and this happened very recently (from a friend of mine who is not a client) – "What is your view on Bitcoin and Cryptocurrency?"

My response is always framed in similar words to those of Stephen Covey, the American educator: "Let's seek first to understand what exactly is on offer here." There are several questions you should ask before taking up any investment opportunity. I like to use these questions to get people to explain the potential investment back to me.

These questions are:

- Is the provider regulated by the FCA?

- If guarantees are on offer, are they contractual and enforceable?

- What are the exact investment terms and conditions?

- How can you get your money back and what is the process?

- What is the partial withdrawal position?

- What are the charges?

- What is the risk?

- Where precisely is the capital invested?

- Is the investment diversified?

- Is the investment legal and ethical, and does it fit with your core values?

- What is the investment term?

- Why do you want to make this investment?

- Is the investment socially responsible and environmentally friendly? (I will discuss this further in Chapter 7.)

In the case of my friend who was asking about Bitcoin and Cryptocurrency, he was able to tell me that he'd bought one Bitcoin for £200 in 2014 and that now (2021) it was worth around £40,000, that he knew the market well and was keen on further Bitcoin investments. On the face of it this sounds like a fantastic investment opportunity, but it is still highly speculative as the market is highly volatile and currently unregulated in the UK. In this instance, I talked to my friend in broad terms, without offering advice or looking into his overall circumstances. I pointed out the volatility and liquidity risk and discussed the merits of him perhaps taking some profit and diversifying.

As regards Bitcoin and Cryptocurrency as an investment, I have very limited knowledge of this new and very specialist area. I would say that detailed research is required to completely understand this new investment entity and only then, as part of a balanced portfolio, would I suggest you consider it. I have not invested the time to fully understand it so I will not be investing anytime soon and I advise my clients to proceed cautiously.

Often the maxim "If it sounds too good to be true, it probably is" holds true. There is a complete difference between investing and speculating.

For example, I like to have a bet on the Grand National every year. I'll put maybe £10 or £20 on a horse and I have had the odd winner. However, I'm not going to put down a £5,000 bet on the National anytime soon – yes at, say, 20/1 I can collect a quick £100,000 if the horse wins, but the likelihood is the horse will not win and why completely ruin my weekend and wipe out my current account balance and then some? Buying a share on a tip from a mate down the pub is arguably no different from gambling on the Grand National. Investing in any unresearched opportunity is speculating rather than investing.

When you are presented with an investment opportunity, you have to understand precisely the underlying vehicle and provider that you're investing in. You need to understand everything from what the asset class is to how the investment actually works.

The key is to understand the **real** assets that you're investing in.

When it comes to understanding what you're investing in, it's also important to be return-realistic. For example, at the time of writing, cash accounts in the UK will yield a return of well under one per cent net whereas a well-diversified balanced fund portfolio held over the requisite minimum five years should deliver annually between four and six per cent.

When deciding which investments to invest in and seeking to decipher whether or not you fully understand it, ask yourself this question: what is my desired return and when will I need the money back? Often, when we are presented with this fantastic investment opportunity offering some spectacular return, we are fuelled either by greed, the fear of missing out or a sense of duty because our close friend who we know, like and trust has also invested. Is that close friend an investment expert or fund manager? Remember rule number three: invest primarily to beat inflation. In my experience, most clients simply want to comfortably beat inflation over the long term without taking undue risk.

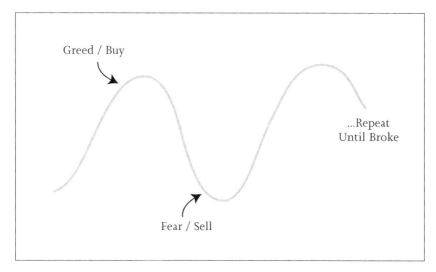

Speculating: an emotional rollercoaster

Understanding your investments, and indeed their liquidity positions, highlights the importance of diversifying your investments as well. For example, if you had invested all of your money in one commercial property fund before 2020 and in early 2020 when the Covid-19 pandemic hit you needed to withdraw some or all of that money, you could have (depending on the fund provider) found it very difficult, if not impossible. This is because the pandemic (and the shift from the office to home-working), and the resulting temporary closure of the high street, forced commercial property fund managers to re-evaluate their positions. The result of this was that many providers suspended their commercial property funds. When a fund is suspended, there can be no inflows and no outflows/withdrawals. In an extreme example, if you had your investments in one commercial property fund and it were to be suspended, access to capital for lump sums or income would be impossible until the suspension lifts, which can take many months.

This is also a potential issue with highly illiquid infrastructure funds, so it is vital that you understand the liquidity position of all your investments. It is for this reason that I advise my clients typically not to hold more than 10–15 per cent of their money in any one fund.

Howard's story

During the dot-com bubble of the early 2000s, I remember myself buying a few dot-com shares at £500 per share. Internet share trading was in its infancy at this time, and I excitedly bought one dot-com share for around 50p, and within a day or so it was worth about 150p.

Out of sheer greed and riding on media hype, I held on, hopeful of even more profit. Of course, the dot-com bubble fairly quickly burst and I lost everything invested. Now, I did, however, remember not to speculate with money I could not afford to lose and while the circa £2,000–£2,500 losses were painful, it was not my life savings I put on the line. Did I fully under-stand the dot-com share market and how the underlying share was capitalised? NO! I was motivated by hype and greed and I ended up with a bloody nose, but I fancied a "punt" and I lived to tell the tale as I did not take too big an investment position.

This demonstrates the importance of understanding the underlying investment you are making. As well as knowing how share trading works, you also need to know about the companies whose shares you are buying, to help you assess the potential risks and to be real-istic about your potential returns. The examples I have shared here are speculating, rather than investing, and I'm not saying that people can't make a lot of money from speculating. However, I have seen (and I'm sure you're also aware of) some horror stories where people lose substantial amounts of money speculating.

The key is to understand what you are putting your money into, so that you can make an informed decision about whether that risk really is acceptable to you. If you don't understand an investment opportunity, go to a financial adviser who can help you understand it.

This all said, often a client will invest in their passion for sport, a hobby or an interest. I have clients who have put money into horse ownership, art and paintings, watch collections and classic cars amongst other things (I call this the sixth asset class as mentioned earlier) and not only have some of them made good returns, but along the way they have enjoyed the ownership thrill and, after all, isn't that what life is all about?

In addition to ensuring you understand what you are investing in, it is equally important to avoid the temptation to "time" the markets. When markets have just fallen, clients have often said to me: "Let's wait on your proposal to invest until the market stabilises." Waiting in this instance is probably the wrong thing to do – if the market falls, then at this point an investor buys their asset-backed fund investment at a cheaper price.

As long as you adhere to rule five and hold for the long term, you may have bought the investment cheaply but you are more likely to see its value rise.

That said, many times I have recommended to a client who is concerned about the general stock market falling that we phase or drip the investment into the plan over a period of often three, six or up to 12 months. We do this by moving the investment from an initial cash holding fund each month into the designated investment portfolio. This way, IF the market does fall, my client benefits from buying into a falling market (where the units are cheaper as they are worth less) and therefore has not bought all of their investment before the fall, at a higher price.

The golden rules of investing in practice

Let's look at a real scenario and how following the golden rules of investment would help you in that situation.

4 Statista, (2022), 'FTSE 100 Index UK from December 2019 to December 2021', Statista, 31 January, available at: https://www.statista.com/statistics/1103739/ftse-100-index-uk/

Between 12 February and 23 March 2020, in a blind panic reaction to the breaking news of the Covid-19 pandemic, the FTSE 100 suffered falls from 7,534.37 to 4,993.89[4], an alarming 33.72 per cent drop, before steadily recovering to 7,347.91 on 12 November 2021, around 20 months later. In 2020 as a whole, the vast majority of my clients' portfolios saw positive growth despite this upset.

Firstly, you stuck to rule number one, and **didn't borrow to invest**, so you haven't put yourself under undue financial pressure. You've followed rule number two, so **you have enough cash** that you don't need to liquidate your investments and you can ride out this volatility. You're also sticking to rule number five, that you've **invested for the long term**, so again you are prepared to hold your investments, and you know the markets will bounce back. Following rule number three, to **invest primarily to beat inflation**, means you won't panic about how markets recover, because your returns need to outpace inflation and anything beyond that is a bonus.

If you have also stuck to rule number four and diversified your investments across asset classes, then the stock market won't be the only place where your money is invested and therefore a fall in the stock market won't necessarily impact your entire portfolio, which is well balanced and diversified. If you have also stuck to rule number six, and found the best people to manage your money, then you will be confident that your investments are in safe hands and know that you don't have to actively watch what is happening because you have a team of the best people doing that for you.

Finally, you **understand your underlying investments,** and how they behave during times of extreme volatility, which gives you peace of mind about your strategy and helps you to make rational decisions, rather than reacting emotionally to shock headlines.

From an investment perspective, you can't go far wrong if you follow the seven golden rules of investment, as you can see from this example.

Summary

After reading these first two chapters, you can hopefully understand why it is important to look at service, advice and performance when you are making a decision about whether or not to engage a financial adviser. The seven golden rules of investment give you a strong growth foundation, not only for making investments if you decide to do it all yourself but also for finding a financial adviser who can support you.

This first part of the book is designed to give you a solid understanding of the fields of financial advice and investment growth management, as well as how this advice and investment management is intergenerational. We will then build on this as we move into more specific detail around estate planning in Part 2 and then creating your own financial plan in Part 3.

Part 2:

Estate Planning Stories (Pass It On)

This part of the book is essentially about growing diversified wealth, and part of that involves avoiding tax and beating inflation. What I won't do in this book is tell you how to spend your money; however, I will approach these chapters with the great hope that the money you make will be spent ethically, morally and for both your and your family's benefit and enjoyment so that you live a very happy and fulfilled life.

Achieving financial independence and understanding how much is needed is another crucial element of estate planning. Everyone has a different "golden number" in terms of how much they are going to need when they retire to last them for the rest of their lives. Some of the chapters in this part of the book will cover topics that people typically don't want to talk about, such as wills and later life care. However, while no one wants to talk about dying or living with dementia, going into a nursing home or substituted decision making, the fact is that you may need nursing or residential care as you get older, and I'm sorry to say this but none of us will last forever.

I have a qualification from the Society of Later Life Advisers (SOLLA) because I believe it's incredibly important for a financial adviser to have in-depth knowledge about this important stage in all of our lives. Intergenerational advice is particularly key because it isn't only you who could benefit from my advice, but also your children, nieces, nephews and other family members who are part of the next generation.

If your parents are still with us, they could also benefit from advice. Through my personal experiences with my own beloved parents, and the SOLLA qualification, I can empathise with your whole family. I can understand what you or your parents will be going through as they get older, and I can also understand what you, your children and the rest of your family will be going through, not only from a financial perspective but also from an emotional one, having been there myself. Understanding family across all generations is essential to enable me to provide the best possible advice, not only for you but your entire family.

I also want to highlight a crucial point when we are discussing wills, LPA, estate succession planning and inheritance tax mitigation – remember, we are not talking about a particularly nice topic here; effectively, we are planning for our future demise and merely in doing so trying to keep things as simple and tax efficient for our next generation as we possibly can.

So well done to you for seeking to learn more about and navigate through this subject – many of your peers will either refuse to think about it or at best do very little about it. YOU are part of the courageous few.

I'm going to start by looking at one of the most important documents you will write in your life: your will.

Chapter 3:

Wills

"I have noticed even people who claim everything is predestined, and that we can do nothing to change it, look before they cross the road."

– Stephen Hawking[5]

5 Stephen Hawking, (1994), Black Holes and Baby Universes and Other Essays, Bantam, paperback edition

Firstly, I am not a solicitor, will writer or legal professional of any kind and I am not qualified to write your will. As part of my chartered financial planner qualification, I have, however, passed a Society of Trust and Estate Practitioners' (STEP) "STEP Certificate for Financial Services", which has helped me over the years to understand the importance of robust will and estate planning and why it is vital to support the client relationship by working closely with suitably qualified legal professionals.

Therefore, whenever I meet a new client, as part of my first meeting process I always ask them if they have a will. If the answer is "no" then I recommend as a first step, before they even consider their financial planning, that they sit down with a qualified solicitor or STEP-qualified will writer as soon as possible. If you die without a will, it is known as dying intestate, and the laws of intestacy in the UK are, at best, complicated, especially where your own circumstances are complex, and, at worst, could cause an unwelcome inheritance tax bill.

If you are reading this and you don't have a will, I urge you to write one as soon as possible. To be blunt, we simply don't know when we're going to "leave the party" and, as Benjamin Franklin said: "In this world, nothing can be said to be certain, except death and taxes." The other questions I ask my clients about their wills are who the executors and main beneficiaries are. This is important as, if I am to forge a long-term client relationship, I need to know who is responsible for their estate when they pass away, and also where the money is then headed and to whom.

A will is the cornerstone of sound financial planning and arguably more important than having a financial plan. UK intestacy laws say that, if you're married or in a civil partnership, your spouse will automatically receive only a proportion of your estate upon your death. Currently, they would retain all assets (including property) up to £270,000 and all personal possessions, in addition to an absolute interest in 50 per cent of the remainder, with the other half divided equally between the surviving children. Is that what you want to happen? I doubt it, so make a will which reflects your exact wishes and use a qualified professional to do so.

I did highlight in my introduction on this subject that you are part of the "courageous few" who are seeking to do the right thing in having your estate affairs in order – as further proof of this, staggeringly, according to research by Oratto[6], 61 per cent of British adults do not have a will, which equates to a whopping 30 million people.

What do you need to know about writing a will?

Firstly, no matter how old you are (that is, once you're over the age of 18), it's very important that you have a will. This still applies if you're a single person with no dependants because the reality is that you will have assets and you will want to pass those in the right direction, whether that's to family, friends or charity.

Simply having a basic will where, as a married person, you leave everything to your spouse and then to your children can be sufficient for many clients. Your will, however, should be professionally written using a qualified solicitor who specialises in wills and probate work or a will writer who is qualified by STEP and has passed at least the STEP Certificate in Trusts and Estates/ Will Preparation. Will writing firms are not regulated by the Law Society, so it is important you check that

6 Oratto, (2018), '30 million adults in Britain do not have a Will', 23 July, available at: https://oratto.co.uk/blog/wills/30-million-adults-in-britain-do-not-have-a-will

you have someone with the necessary professional qualifications and experience. One of the most important elements of writing a will is its attestation, or the signing/witnessing of the will, which (even with a basic will) is easy to get wrong. This is why using a suitably qualified professional is essential, as, in the event of a problem, you have their professional indemnity insurance to fall back on.

As I said at the beginning of this chapter, and I know that I am a cheery soul and that talking about our demise is not usually top of most people's agenda, the fact is that we don't know when we are going to "leave the party", so make a will because it is a reflection of your wishes right now. You can always change your will and this is relatively straightforward to do. There are two main ways to alter your will: the first is a redraft or a full rewrite of your will, which means your previous will becomes redundant as the new will has a clause added renouncing all previous wills; the second is by adding a codicil to your will, which can supplement, modify or revoke part or all of your will.

Writing a will isn't a difficult process with the right professional support, and it is a task you shouldn't procrastinate over. I often see a new or existing client who says to me: "Yes, I will get around to doing my will, Howard, but I doubt I will be dying this year so I will leave it for now." If you are looking at your financial planning then, in tandem, this is the perfect opportunity to either update or complete your will if you don't already have one.

Choosing your executors wisely

When you write a will, you will have to choose executors, whose job is to execute and administer your wishes contained within the will. There are a few things to bear in mind when making your selection, the first being that you trust them to do a good job for you. Secondly, they should ideally be local to you, or within a reasonable travelling distance; however, in this virtual world of ours this is maybe no longer so important. They also have to understand the importance of the job because being an executor requires quite a lot of administrative work and they will need to follow through on certain actions. If they have some financial acumen, that is also very useful. It might also be an idea to appoint people who are younger than you as you will need them to be around after you have left the party.

If you appoint two or three executors in your will, it's essential they understand they are working together for the common good to execute your wishes. Although executors are often close family members or friends, you can also appoint a firm of solicitors as executor if you don't have anyone who falls into this category or if you feel that your executors could use professional help due to their ages, health, location etc. Be careful when you are choosing a solicitor firm as an executor though and be sure you understand the cost of their services. My advice would be to ask for a fixed fee. (This is my advice whenever you are dealing with solicitors/ accountants/tax experts and indeed any fellow profes-sional – can you negotiate a fixed fee? That way, there are never any unwanted financial fee surprises.)

Nothing comes for free...

When, in 2006, a married couple from Barnard Castle who attended my investment and estate planning seminar first came to me, they told me that they had a will with their bank, which had been written entirely free of charge. They were happy with its contents and felt that it reflected their wishes. However, all was not quite what it seemed. I asked who the executors of their will were and the response was, "the bank". I asked how much the bank would charge for their probate administration services and they couldn't tell me.

It took a lot of digging, but eventually we got to the bottom of the bank's fee structure for administering their wills as professional executors. The couple in question had a total estate value of around £600,000, and the bank would have charged them a whopping six per cent of their estate value (£36,000) for probate services! Needless to say, they quickly called upon a local firm of solicitors and paid the firm's competitive upfront fee to rewrite their wills, naming their grown-up children as the executors of their estate. The point here is that the bank offered a "free" will writing service, but wanted to be named as the professional executors because of the fee ability for probate services upon the day of reckoning. Be wary of any such "free" offer.

Why not go down the DIY will writing route?

It is possible to walk into a high-street store (WHSmith often gets a mention) and buy a will writing kit for very little money and do-it-yourself. The opposite of the Nike catchphrase "Just **don't** do it" resonates here for me. It is so easy to get it wrong on many fronts; your will is arguably THE most important document you will EVER write, so use a professional who specialises in this area.

There are two main reasons why I recommend working with experienced solicitors or STEP-qualified will writers. The first is that these people have written hundreds of wills in their time, and if you engage someone who has good empathy and the necessary softer people skills, you will benefit from this as well as their sound technical expertise. Secondly, as mentioned, they will hold professional indemnity insurance, so if there are any issues down the line your estate will be protected.

The key is to find a good firm of solicitors or will writers to work with, and this is why I recommend looking for those who are STEP-qualified specialists in estate planning and probate work. It can be particularly beneficial if you have a complicated estate because a good, well-qualified solicitor or will writer will cut through that complexity and ensure that you end up with the right solution. Let me give you a flavour of the work they can do...

Protection against "sideways disinheritance"

The beneficiaries of your will are the people who will inherit your assets. For many married couples or civil partnerships, it is common practice to set up immediate post death interest (IPDI) trusts to protect against a "sideways disinheritance".

For example, Bob and Jill are married and have two sons. Let's say Bob passes away when their joint estate is worth £500,000. He wanted his half of the estate (£250,000) to go to his two sons when he passed, so he had set up an IPDI in his will. On his death, his half share of the estate goes into the IPDI trust, protecting his sons' inheritance so that, were Jill to remarry in future, rather than the whole of Bob's half share passing directly to Jill, his £250,000 is protected so that only his sons and Jill can benefit via the IPDI trust and not Jill's new partner.

Professional will writing/legal advice is needed here. This is not a specific area I am able or qualified sufficiently to advise upon; neither are will trusts.

Other will trusts

These can take various forms such as a discretionary trust that takes up to the inheritance tax (IHT) nil rate band or IPDI trusts with added discretionary flexibility for the capital (a flexible life interest trust or FLIT). These are often recommended by the STEP solicitor/ will writer where a married couple or civil partnership have an IHT bill on second demise. The advantages in doing so are numerous, but some are as follows:

- With the FLIT, gifts to beneficiaries can be made from the will trust, which then become potentially exempt transfers (PETs) and are removed from the survivor's estate upon seven years' survival.

- With both trusts, the trust fund can be accessed by the trustees on second death to meet a potential IHT bill, avoiding the need for the executors to borrow to pay it – this could be a key benefit.

What about property?

Many couples in the UK jointly own property in standard "joint tenancy" terms, meaning that if I pass away first my wife automatically owns the property, irrespective of what the will says, because the property does not pass through the will in these circumstances as only sole assets pass into your will. It is possible, however, to still have joint ownership of this property but instead own it on a "tenants' in common" (TIC) basis – often referred to as "severing the tenancy from joint tenancy". The effect here is that each owner usually has a 50 per cent outright ownership (sole) which, from an estate planning perspective, means that this 50 per cent share can be directed via their will. Often this 50 per cent share is added to the will trust as described previously to protect against sideways disinheritance.

Over the years, I have met a number of clients who tell me they have set up a main residence property trust through a solicitor or, more commonly, an unqualified will writer. The purpose of the trust is to ring-fence the whole of their main residence as being outside of their or their partner's estate to avoid it being included within the local authority financial assessment as regards long-term care payments.

Clients who take this approach need to be careful they do not fall foul of the "deliberate deprivation of assets" rule. Where property is distributed with the deliberate intention of avoiding a long-term care bill, the local authority can call the "deprived" property back and it can be re-included as part of the assets within the financial assessment. I'll talk more about this in the section on long-term care in Chapter 6. Personally, I'm not a great fan of trusts to protect your main residential property in this way because they could be open in future to a challenge by the local authority for deliberate deprivation unless there is a clear rationale as to why the property has been applied this way. The quality and strength (in the event of a challenge) of the legal advice you receive is therefore vital here.

Keep it simple

I am not a qualified solicitor or will writer, and some estate planning, will writing and trust planning solutions can be complex, so as a theme running through this book I urge you to not only take the time to fully understand your financial and estate planning but also ensure that your executors/trustees and beneficiaries have a similar understanding.

Involve the next generation

It is always better to involve the next generation when you are writing your will and carrying out estate planning. I recommend involving your executors/trustees and beneficiaries so long as you feel comfortable in doing so – when the time does come for you to pass on the baton of responsibility, it's then a seamless transition which they can understand and fulfil with the help of their chartered financial planner, solicitor/will writer and any other professional you have introduced them to.

The aim is always to pass wealth from one generation to the next in a tax-efficient manner and to avoid any nasty shocks. Involving the next generation can work very well; I would commend it to you.

I can think of one instance in particular where, because a large family had not clearly communicated their clear beneficial and financial wishes during their parents' lifetime, the parents' estate took a number of years to settle, with the resultant stress and anxiety taking a toll on the whole family.

Intergenerational engagement, understanding and clear communication with professional guidance can ensure instead that a complex estate can be swiftly and tax efficiently administered.

Lasting power of attorney (LPA)

This is another area where the services of a legal professional are necessary. I always advise my clients to make an LPA at the same time that they make their will. Like a will, you will need to do this through your solicitor or STEP-qualified will writer – it isn't a service that a chartered financial planner can offer directly.

An LPA states who you want to manage your estate in the event that you lose the mental capacity to do so. You are the donor of the power and you appoint attorneys who will act on your behalf. None of us know if or when we may lose mental capacity and with the prevalence of dementia in modern society, it is certainly important to consider.

If you create an LPA in your 20s or 30s, it will be in place for the rest of your life and you won't have to worry about doing it when you are older and potentially reaching a stage where you could be considered to have lost capacity. Whatever age you are, my question is always: "Why wait?" It's the same cost to do it now as it will be when you're 70, 80 or 90 even, so there is no reason not to put this in place – look upon it as an insurance policy to your loved ones.

If you don't have an LPA and you lose mental capacity, in England and Wales your incapacity situation will be referred to the Office of the Public Guardian (an office within the Court of Protection) and they will appoint a deputy to manage your affairs – this can take time and involves a financial cost. When this happens, there are no guarantees that the Office of the Public Guardian will appoint who you want as your attorney. For example, I know that personally I would want either my wife and/or my two adult sons to manage my financial and personal affairs in this instance. I would also want them to be appointed swiftly and without administration and financial burden at what would be a difficult time for everyone – my LPA allows just this.

Your legal professional is the expert on these important documents and powers – they have the depth of knowledge to cover your questions on any aspect of the Mental Capacity Act 2005, which underpins lasting power of attorney legislation.

What is the difference between enduring power of attorney and LPA?

LPA was introduced in 2007 following on from the Mental Capacity Act 2005; before this, enduring power of attorney (EPA) legislation applied. The EPA is still a valid instrument; however, if you do have an EPA talk to your legal professional about the differences to the LPA legislation. EPA powers are narrower and do not cover health and welfare decisions, whereas LPAs allow your loved ones to make medical, health and welfare decisions on your behalf as well as financial decisions.

Another key difference between the two is that an EPA must be registered when the donor loses mental capacity and not before. LPAs, however, can be registered immediately and the property and affairs LPA (which I'll explain next) can be used whether or not the donor has mental capacity.

The two types of LPA

There are two types of LPA: property and affairs LPA and health and welfare LPA.

Property and affairs:
With this LPA, the attorney is able to act for the donor in financial matters and make financial decisions on their behalf without the donor having lost mental capacity. The attorney must act, of course, in the donor's best interests at all times – this power can be useful to the family where the donor has capacity but is physically infirm and therefore perhaps unable to visit their bank, allowing the attorneys to, for example, take a safety deposit box in and out of the bank or cash/deposit a cheque and so on.

Personal welfare:
This allows the attorneys, as the name suggests, to make medical and welfare decisions on behalf of the donor. In this case, the donor must have lost mental capacity for the attorneys to act. Substituted decision making in this area can be complex and your appointed legal person can help and advise your family at the time of need.

Choosing your attorney(s)

It's essential to choose an attorney (or attorneys, as you can have more than one) who you trust to execute your wishes. If you are appointing more than one attorney, there are two options: joint or joint and several.

When the donor appoints joint attorneys, all of them have to act unanimously. When you have joint and several attorneys, one of them can act on behalf of the other attorneys. For example, if you have four children, but only one who lives locally, you might appoint all of them as attorneys under a joint and several arrangement – the local child can then act and make decisions without having to constantly ask their siblings for permission as would be the case with the joint attorney appointment.

Use a professional to set up an LPA

Just like with your will, I strongly recommend that you use a solicitor or STEP-qualified will writer to create your LPA.

I believe that the money you pay a professional to create your LPA is more than worth it. You can set up LPAs yourself online, but be prepared for the hassle of a circa 70-page gov.uk form to contend with. Get any element of the LPA application wrong, in a similar way to getting your will drawn up incorrectly, and this could cause issues for your attorneys at the point the powers are required. Also, remember that when the LPAs are needed the legal professional is there to give you ongoing advice, which can be vital.

My counsel is always to seek professional legal advice because the fees for doing so are, when you choose your appointed firm/adviser wisely, considerably lower than the cost and emotional stress of getting it wrong, or failing to set up LPAs at all.

Howard's story

This is a subject that is very close to me personally, having used both types of LPA for my own father. In 2012, I organised a meeting between myself, my Dad and the STEP-qualified will writer who I work closely with to talk about his will and LPAs.

Even though I had recommended scores of clients set up their wills and LPAs over the years by referring them to a legal professional, doing this for my Dad was not without its challenges. It was certainly a difficult process to go through as a son, as my Dad wasn't always happy about taking advice from his "little boy" (chartered professional or not!), albeit indirectly via STEP-qualified will writer Leah Hamilton of Hamilton Legacy. Leah did, however, thanks in no small part to her excellent empathy and compassion, manage to have a will and both types of LPA set up for us over several meetings with my Dad. I am an only child, so I was named as my Dad's sole attorney for the LPAs, as well as the sole executor and beneficiary for his will.

I first used the property and affairs LPA for my Dad in around 2014 when he needed me to call at his bank to pick up his safe deposit box as he was poorly. At that time he had full mental capacity, the bank accepted my identification and the LPA document and I returned the safety deposit box to Dad and then back to the bank.

In October 2016, my Dad was diagnosed with dementia and in early 2018, following a fall at home which hospitalised him, we decided that he was unsafe in his own home and that he needed full-time residential dementia care. We took the decision to move him straight from hospital to a care home that we selected for him (my wife and I saw three care homes before choosing the best one) and we were able to do this as he was a "self-funder" (he was responsible for his long-term care payments as the financial assets he held were worth more than the minimum limit whereby the local authority instead would fund his care) – more on this funding position in the section later in the book on long-term care.

Dementia is an awful, progressive disease and in the weeks before he died in mid-December 2018, certain medical decisions needed to be made and I was able to make those decisions thanks to the personal welfare power of attorney, as well as taking advice from Leah Hamilton. When he passed away, as the sole executor for his estate, I obtained probate for his estate myself, which was a fairly straightforward process as his estate was not complex. His gift legacies were paid, including two sums that were later put into trust for his two grandsons and I recall Leah helping me here on the finer detail.

Having professionally drafted LPAs and a will in place for my Dad made life much easier for me, as his only son, when faced with some challenging decisions and situations. I have seen the benefit of having these instruments in place first-hand, which is why I am so keen for all of my clients to consider their benefits and do likewise.

Summary

As I said in relation to will writing, I am a chartered financial planner and, although I hold a STEP for Financial Services, Trusts and Estate Planning qualification, I am far from an expert in this field. However, this qualification has helped me realise how vital it is that my clients' wills and LPAs are made a cornerstone of their holistic financial planning, hence why I have highlighted them in some detail here.

The reason I like my clients to have a will and LPAs in place is that it makes it much easier for me to help them with their investment and estate planning position as I know that, firstly, their estate will be distributed in accordance with their wishes and, secondly, their family is protected should mental incapacity occur. In the next chapter, we are going to take an in-depth look at inheritance tax, including exactly what it is, how you can mitigate it and how best to carry out succession planning to your loved ones and next generation

Chapter 4:

Inheritance Tax

"....and to my friends at the Inland Revenue, I leave 40% of my estate."

In 1986, Roy Jenkins, Labour politician and former Chancellor of the Exchequer, said: "Inheritance tax is broadly a voluntary levy paid by those who distrust their heirs more than they dislike the Inland Revenue."

Inheritance Tax and Estate planning, much like wills and LPA, is not a particularly nice and cheery subject to consider as we are, of course, planning for our demise. Therefore, the adviser's role is to empathise accordingly and to ensure we work to your timeframes for its discussion and not our own.

Inheritance tax is a valuable source of income for the UK Treasury, and, given the recent hike in UK property prices added to the cap imposed until 2026 on IHT reliefs and thresholds, you do not need to be ultra-wealthy to have your estate pay it. In the 2020/21 tax year, a whopping £5.32 billion was raised from IHT receipts[7].

It is a somewhat "passive" and also politically non-contentious tax in that if, for example, you are one of three children and are set to inherit one third of your parents' £2 million estate, although there would be a likely IHT

---

7 D. Clark, (2021), 'Inheritance tax receipts in the UK from 2000/01 to 2020/21', Statista, 29 April, available at: https://www.statista.com/statistics/284325/ united-kingdom-hmrc-tax-receipts-inheritance-tax/

bill of £400,000 (assuming both parents' nil rate band and residence nil rate band are available), you will still receive an inheritance of just over £530,000 – not bad, eh? However, and I am with Roy Jenkins here, you have worked hard and paid income tax on the dot all of your life so why allow the Inland Revenue, as the parents of the three children in this example, to be one of the largest beneficiaries of your joint estate when, with some good and timely financial advice and planning, this bill can be partially or fully wiped out?

However, when it comes to inheritance tax you should never take a "sledgehammer" approach to its mitigation. Instead it's all about carefully chipping away at it, each year doing a little bit to mitigate it. Above all, it's essential to take professional advice. Usually I would recommend you start getting advice in this area as you are approaching retirement age and that you continue to take advice on an ongoing annual basis thereafter.

There are many elements to effective inheritance tax mitigation, from using trusts to gifting capital and income to your beneficiaries either during your lifetime or via your will. As Roy Jenkins said, it is largely a voluntary tax, but I have seen many people over the years take the "ostrich" approach, burying their heads in the sand and hoping their beneficiaries will pick up the pieces. Do you really want to leave that legacy?

Do you take the ostrich approach above OR do you plan to instead take professional IHT mitigation advice?

One of the most important things to understand about inheritance tax is that it must be paid before your beneficiaries can access your estate via probate. The question you have to ask yourself is how will your children or other beneficiaries, who perhaps have mortgages and other debts and maybe who aren't wealthy themselves, find the money to pay your IHT bill? Will they have to take out a probate loan with a bank, which not only takes time and costs money, but is also a stressful process for those involved at a tricky and indeed emotional time?

Tax avoidance versus tax evasion

I want to be very clear here: what I am talking about in this book and the advice I provide is there to avoid inheritance tax and certainly NOT to evade inheritance tax. Tax evasion is illegal; tax avoidance is legitimate. Over the years, many times I have heard a prospective client say to me: "What about if I just give my son/daughter some cash or a painting/asset etc – who will know?" My retort to that prospective client is: "You have no doubt been honest and ethical throughout your life – why do you now want to run the risk of being a tax evader? Is this really the legacy you want to leave your family?"

My maxim is always: "There is no such thing as partial honesty." I live my life by this maxim and encourage all clients to do likewise – with good financial advice and careful planning there is NO need to even consider anything other than working only to avoid inheritance tax rather than to evade it.

Also, I want to highlight the importance of keeping good records of your estate value, bank accounts and investment plans held, together with any gifts you have given to your beneficiaries in your lifetime. Details of where your will and LPA are stored and any other wishes you have are also important. I like to provide my clients with a booklet (which we call "My Documents") for these facts and figures to be recorded in, which I encourage them to share with their closest family. In addition, by sharing a confidential copy of this document with our office, when your executors and beneficiaries require our help we have all of this information available so that we can help them liaise with solicitors and other professionals at what will probably be a difficult time for them. This also ensures that the ongoing advice and service they receive is intergenerational.

What I want to show you here is how you solve the problem of an inheritance tax bill by taking tax avoidance advice. I firstly need to fully understand the extent of your inheritance taxable estate, and once I have calculated your IHT liability I can then recommend a plan of action to avoid it.

What is the IHT problem?
A typical but hypothetical client example

Meet Ken and Carole

Ken and Carole are a couple at retirement age. Ken, 62, has just sold his electronics business, paying all the taxes on that sale. Carole, 60, has recently retired from the NHS, taking a tax-free lump sum and her DB pension.

Let's look at their assets to see how their inheritance tax liability might stack up.

• They have a house worth £400,000 (jointly owned)

- They have jointly owned cash assets in various bank accounts of around £600,000 from the sale of Ken's business and Carole's NHS lump sum

- They have a UK holiday home worth £250,000 (jointly owned)

- They have investment ISAs worth around £200,000 (£100,000 each)

- They have shares worth £50,000 (£25,000 each)

- Ken has VCTs worth £100,000

- They have an investment bond worth £50,000 (joint)

- They have personal assets (cars/jewellery/house contents) worth around £200,000

Overall, their estate value is around £1.85 million

From this overall value, they can deduct the applicable nil rate bands.

In this case these are:

- Two inheritance tax nil rate bands (2021/22) of £325,0000 each (totalling £650,000)

- Two private residence nil rate bands (2021/22) of £175,000 each (totalling £350,000)

Total estate = £1,85 million - £1 million (in nil rate bands) = £850,000 that is liable for inheritance tax

Inheritance tax is charged at 40 per cent over the £1 million threshold, which means the following for Ken and Carole's estate:

£850,000 x 40 per cent = £340,000 inheritance tax liability payable on second death

If you look at that example of Ken and Carole, and imagine that they have a large family of five children who are equal beneficiaries in the estate, then HMRC will currently benefit £38,000 more than each of their children's sole inheritances of £302,000 each!!

Later in the chapter we shall return to Ken and Carole with some potential tax planning and gifting solutions to avoid their IHT bill after we have run through some potential outline planning solutions.

What I am going to explore in this chapter are the various ways in which you can mitigate and avoid your inheritance tax liability, looking at some of the pitfalls you may face along the way. We'll start with joining the SKI Club and gifting.

The SKI Club

Me and my wife, Gill, in Austria in early 2020, applying to join the SKI Club!

This was another slide at our investment seminar that received a giggle or two: "Join the SKI Club" was the slide and the question asked was: "What is it?" The answer: the "spend your kids' inheritance club" – **cue roars of laughter...**

Joining the SKI Club can be trickier than you think: you need to spend your cash on consumables, so do that world cruise, fishing holiday to Iceland, two-month holiday to Australia and New Zealand – you have to spend the wealth on items that will actually reduce your estate. Remember, if you spend your money buying expensive Rolex watches or oil paintings, you are just transferring your wealth onto your wrist or onto your wall – the watch and painting are still very much part of your taxable IHT estate. I also find with my clients that rarely does a leopard change its spots, so if you've been a saver your entire life it's tough to turn into a free-spending consumer of luxury items and perishable goods.

I remember one client who came to an investment seminar around 12 years ago seeking advice and I recommended using trusts to save inheritance tax. I provided him with a recommendation and, after giving it some thought, he came to me and said: "What I have actually decided to do is take the £100,000 you have recommended is added to the trust and spend it on a full year's world cruise for myself and my wife." I was delighted for him, so I shook his hand, told him that I thought it was a fantastic idea that he was spending and, more importantly, enjoying his money on a trip of a lifetime, and wished them both a safe and memorable trip.

They came back from their cruise a year or so later and got back in touch; they still had an inheritance tax problem, so we proceeded with a mitigation solution and they remain valued clients to this day.

I am an absolute advocate of you spending your money and living your life to the full. I often suggest to my wife, who is by her own admission fairly frugal, that she should go out, spend and "live a little" (in fact, "live a lot"!) because I can guarantee that if we don't spend it then our sons and our daughters-in-law will! Joking aside, I will often have conversations with my clients about spending more money now, while they are young, fit and healthy so that they can enjoy it – to be brutal – "There are no pockets in shrouds" – so let's try not to be the richest corpse in the graveyard...

Gifting

You can gift money, free from IHT, using a number of standard HMRC gifts and exemptions (see the table later in this section for full details).

When you are gifting over and above these standard exemptions to an individual or to an absolute trust (known as a potentially exempt transfer or PET) or to a discretionary trust (known as a chargeable lifetime transfer), then the **seven-year survival rule** applies. This means that your gifts are IHT-free post seven years survival from the date of the gift. If you die within seven years, the gift will be liable for inheritance tax; however, taper relief may apply on larger gifts, but only on amounts over your £325,000 IHT nil rate band. The rule here also aggregates any other gifts given within potentially a 14-year timeframe – this can now become complex so I do not want to go into too much technical detail here. What I will say is take specific chartered financial planning advice surrounding your gifting and always keep good records of those gifts – your executors will be thankful that you did!

It is also possible to gift your beneficiaries the difference between what you earn and what your normal income and expenditure is and avoid the gifted amounts being included in your estate. So, if you earn, say, £2,000 a month through your pensions, but you only spend £1,500 of that as your normal monthly expenditure, then you can legitimately give £500 to your beneficiaries each month, as long as those gifts are certain in nature, regular in nature (monthly or annually usually) and will not negatively impact your standard of living.

Ultimately, when it comes to gifting, I say give as much away as you are comfortable with but remember:

- You might need it in your lifetime, so not too much!

- Remain as comfortable as possible, and gift as much as you feel is right to your beneficiaries and/ or charity during your lifetime. The rules around gifting can seem complicated, so here is a table to help you better understand how much you can give away before the seven-year survival rule applies.

Gifting Exemptions

Type of Gift	Value	IHT Saving	When Exempt
Small gifts	£250	£100	Immediately
Annual gifts	£3,000	£1,200	Immediately
Wedding gifts*	Up to £5,000	£2,000	Immediately
Regular gifts from income	Unlimited	40%	Immediately
Charity	Unlimited	40%	Immediately

*From parents to children; less if given to grandchildren or anyone else

Potential pitfalls with gifting – gift away, but not too much!!!

However, while gifting can be a good way to reduce your inheritance tax liability, there are some pitfalls to be aware of. Firstly, as I have already said, take care that you are not giving away money that you might need yourself in your lifetime. It sounds harsh but you have no guarantee that your children, or whoever the beneficiaries are, will give it back. Secondly, you have to consider what your beneficiaries might spend the money on if you gift it to them now.

For example, let's say my and my wife Gill's joint IHT taxable estate is £1.35 million when I reach age 65 (I am 56 today). So, on second death £350,000 would be liable for IHT at 40 per cent, a nice £140,000 windfall for the HMRC. Now, I have two sons: Alex, who is currently aged 24, and Euan, who is aged 14. Let's leap ten years into the future and, with me now being aged 66, Gill and I decide to gift the boys £175,000 each. We are both in good health and confident that we will both survive the magic seven years in order to remove the full £350,000 which is caught for IHT from our joint estate. "Perfect," I hear you say or, "What could possibly go wrong?" Well, in ten years' time, Euan is aged 24 and loves his fast cars and the finer things in life – he blows the lot, much to Mum and Dad's dismay.

Alex is now 34. He married when he was 28 and unfortunately the marriage is now on the rocks. The £175,000 gift is a welcome boost to our estranged daughter-in-law – if they then subsequently divorce, she walks off with half of her ex-mum and dad-in-law's gift to Alex: a cool £87,500. Happily, there is a solution: instead of giving these gifts outright, if they were made into trust, the proceeds would be outside of the boys' estates if they divorce or become bankrupt and, importantly, Gill and I can control when and how they benefit from the trust proceeds – more about the usage of trusts in this way later in this chapter. This advice to gift into trust rather than outright can be life-changing for the family and, with divorce rates in the UK at around one in two or one in three, certainly something to discuss with your financial planner!

Gifting to charities

One point on charities and leaving a legacy to charities is that all gifts to charities are inheritance tax free. Also, I recommend you think about whether, instead of directly leaving a gift to specific charities in your will, you could consider leaving either your lifetime or post-death legacy through an organisation called the Charitable Aid Foundation (CAF). If you have an IHT problem and you leave everything to a registered charity, over and above the standard threshold bands of £325,000 (nil rate band) and up to £175,000 (private residence nil rate band), then you pay no IHT. Also, if you were to leave 10 per cent or more of your estate to charity then the IHT rate payable drops from 40 per cent to 36 per cent.

For example, let's say you leave £150,000 to three charities specifically named in your will. When you pass away, those charities will (in my experience) be keen to receive those gifts as soon as possible, so much so that this can result in unnecessary stress for your estate executors and beneficiaries who are keen to do the right thing but are time pressured by the charities' demand for their cash.

If instead you were to use the CAF, which is an independent organisation, that £150,000 legacy will pass to them in the first instance and they will then distribute £50,000 in a professional and timely manner to each of the three named charities. By using the CAF, you essentially create a buffer between your executors/ beneficiaries and the charities in question, while still ensuring that your chosen charities receive their gifts.

You don't have to wait until you pass away to make a gift to your chosen charities. You can donate while you are alive through the CAF and set up your very own Lifetime Charitable Trust. This will also allow you to witness first-hand the positive impact that your money will have on your chosen charities and may have a life-changing effect for you as you see the joy that your capital can bring. I would like to see more of my wealthier clients take this up – the real-time financial boost to their chosen charities, along with the benefit to their own mental health by helping their charities in their lifetime instead of when they have passed away, could be incredibly rewarding.

Products and trusts available to avoid inheritance tax

After we have used our standard gifting exemptions as outlined, gifted away the money we are comfortable to pass on (bearing in mind the pitfalls of gifting to our beneficiaries outright) and have set up charitable legacies either during our lifetime or on death, there are a number of IHT products and trust solutions available to the chartered financial planner.

I only want to summarise these options briefly. If you buy a BMW, Audi or Ford, you would probably be bored if the salesperson explained every finer point of how the engine works. It is no different here and I want to keep it simple (that theme again!) and brief and give you a "taster" of what is available. I am going to strongly caveat that, before I recommend any of these solutions to my client, I must first of all thoroughly understand their circumstances and risk profile and have explained the products and associated fee and projection illustrations, reflecting back their understanding, so that I am content, in line with FCA guidelines, that the solution and recommendation presented is absolutely the right thing for them and that they fully understand it.

Business Property Relief (BPR) solutions

Broadly, BPR products are of higher risk profile as a general rule; however, they benefit from the fact that, after just two years' survival, the whole amount invested is outside of the client's estate from an IHT perspective. There are a multitude of BPR solutions and providers available. Because of their higher risk nature, care needs to be taken with regards to how much capital is added to the products. Yet, as part of a balanced portfolio, they can present an excellent and, from a survival time perspective, short-term IHT solution, especially where an elderly client or a client in poor health is not confident they will survive the seven years required for outright gifting or gifting into trust solutions.

One or two of my clients have invested, without my advice, directly into commercial woodland and forestry, which can qualify for 100 per cent BPR from IHT (section 104 IHT). Not only is this an environmentally friendly investment, but the commercial occupation of woodland is also free of income and corporation tax. In addition, there is no capital gains tax from the sale of any felled trees – this investment is a consideration for a large investment portfolio to aid diversification.

Term assurance – gift inter-vivos plans

As I've explained, under the seven-year survival rule if you gift money it is still classed as being part of your estate until that seven-year mark from the gift date has passed (this type of gift is called a potentially exempt transfer). So, if you die within the seven years, the gift will be liable for IHT. A gift inter-vivos term assurance life policy is the solution here. The cover needed is the amount of the gift and the term is, of course, written for seven years. Therefore, if you die within seven years the gift is covered via the plan. Again, it is vital that this plan is written in trust and the financial planner helps with a bespoke recommendation which is medically underwritten.

Using your will to mitigate inheritance tax

I talked extensively in the previous chapter about the importance of having a professionally drafted will, and this is particularly the case when it comes to inheritance tax mitigation. For example, for a married couple or a registered civil partnership, you can use both a will trust (to utilise the first to die's IHT nil rate band) and an interest in possession trust for your half of the estate, in your will, to help mitigate your inheritance tax risk.

I am not an expert in this area, but a STEP-qualified will writer or solicitor will be able to advise you and set this up. Here's an example to show you how this could work though.

If you are a married couple, in setting up both a discretionary will trust and an interest in possession trust, the planning opportunities are:

- The IHT bill can be paid from the trust proceeds.

- Gifts can be made from the trusts on
  first death and, upon seven-year survival,
  are outside the estate for IHT.

Trusts and inheritance tax planning

Trust usage becomes important when seeking to mitigate IHT and to protect your loaned or gifted assets.

Parties to a trust are the settlor (typically my client who is using their monies to add to the trust), the trustees (minimum of one trustee appointed but I prefer at least two; these are usually family members and they are the legal owners of the trust capital but must act in the best interests of the beneficiaries) and the beneficiaries, who are usually firstly the spouse and then the children of the settlor in the case of a single settlor trust.

Absolute and discretionary trusts

There are generally two types of trust that are used for inheritance tax mitigation: discretionary and absolute trusts.

Discretionary trusts, as their name implies, offer maximum discretionary powers and flexibility for the settlor. The settlor can appoint and dismiss trustees and beneficiaries at any time, which is useful if there is a family dispute or disagreement or if a new trustee needs to be appointed in substitution for another. Any gifts made to a discretionary trust are known as chargeable lifetime transfers (CLTs) and the seven-year rule applies, as opposed to PETs when gifts are made to individuals or to an absolute trust.

Discretionary trusts have a wide class of beneficiaries to choose from (excluding the settlor) and as the beneficiaries do not have any entitlement to the trust funds then it does not form part of their estate on divorce or bankruptcy. This flexibility comes at a price as there is potential of lifetime IHT tax charge payable on entry: if more capital than the trust's £325,000 threshold is added, a ten-yearly periodic (and a possible exit) charge applies – again, advice here becomes important in both setting up and managing the trust.

Absolute trusts, also known as bare trusts, offer no such flexibility. Beneficiaries and trustees are nominated at the outset and cannot be changed. The absolute trust does have a place, however, when beneficiaries are certain (often used for a parent or grandparent setting money aside for their minor children, which can be an excellent solution, particularly for grandparents where more than the child's Junior ISA limit is to be gifted) or when gifting to avoid IHT for amounts in excess of £325,000.

Trust protection

One of the key benefits of using trusts is to ring-fence the trust capital to your beneficiaries to protect them against potential divorce or bankruptcy scenarios. Let's look at an example to show you what I mean.

Trust protection advantage

Robert has two sons and he sets up a discretionary gift trust with £100,000. When he dies, this trust fund is valued at £150,000. His two sons are named as beneficiaries and the trust remains outside of their estates. If one of Robert's sons subsequently divorces, the money in that trust is ring-fenced from his estranged spouse and can't be included in any divorce settlement.

Given that, as already mentioned, approximately one in two or three marriages in the UK ends in divorce, this is certainly worth considering.

Trust usage is an excellent way to pass on your wealth to only your beneficiaries and not a trustee in bankruptcy or an estranged spouse and, coupled with the right and regular advice, can be an extremely tax-efficient and relatively simplistic way to pass money on to your loved ones.

Investment bonds within a trust

Trustee investment bonds (TIBs) are an excellent tax planning and, when needed, income distribution tool. They allow tax paid (onshore) or tax-free (offshore) income flexibility. I will always appoint younger lives assured onto the bonds (children or even grandchildren), as this affords a seamless succession to pass onto the next generation. As investment bonds can be assigned to beneficiaries, accessing the capital later on can be done extremely tax efficiently; again, this is where both financial planning advice and service become vital, as well as ideally knowing the next generation.

It is important to work with a qualified and experienced financial planner to set up and manage your trusts to ensure that there isn't an overly heavy administrative burden placed on yourself, your beneficiaries or the trustees. I have had one client who, before we met, had set up unit trusts within his Discounted Gift Trust with a competitor firm/adviser. This triggered the need for annual trustee meetings and submission of an annual tax return for the trust, as well as having to account for the tax. Had a TIB been added to the trust instead, the administration would have been so much easier.

When it comes to accessing the trust proceeds either during your lifetime or upon death, and distributing the capital to your beneficiaries, advice and service become extremely important.

A brief overview of the styles of trust available for IHT planning

Loan trusts

Loan trusts are a very flexible way to both enjoy an income and have access to the trust capital (as monies added are not gifted) and can be a useful way of starting a client's IHT mitigation journey.

Usually a discretionary loan trust is set up with a TIB added to it. The cash introduced into the bond is effectively "loaned" to the trustees and therefore any growth is not in the settlor's estate for IHT purposes. Typically, an onshore TIB is used with a flexible tax paid income option in line with investment bond income rules. Any income taken (and spent) is a further reduction on the client's estate from an IHT perspective.

Another important flexibility aspect of a loan trust is the ability to convert it to a gift trust (see definition in the next paragraph), so that the seven-year clock starts ticking from the waiver date, thereby removing the trust proceeds from the client's estate for IHT. This is achieved by the loan trust settlor "waiving" the underlying loan within the trust via a simple deed and is typically used as a client gets older and is happy to forego the loan trust capital access flexibility in favour of the ability to completely remove the trusts proceeds from their estate via the gifting route.

Discounted Gift Trust/Plan (DGP)

Typically I recommend setting this up as a discretionary trust, provided the gift (after the IHT upfront discount) is under £325,000 to avoid the relevant property regime taxation position as described earlier. As with the loan trust, a DGP will have either an onshore or offshore TIB added to it dependent upon my client's tax paying status.

A DGP gives both an immediate IHT saving on the amount introduced, as well as the whole proceeds being removed from your estate after a seven-year survival period. HMRC will allow the settlor, who must be aged 60 or more at the outset, a "discount" which is medically and individually underwritten and is linked to the settlor's age, health and smoking status. The upfront discount offered is typically around 50 per cent of capital introduced and, of course, the whole capital amount added is outside the estate after seven years' survival.

HMRC will provide this discount based firstly upon the settlor demonstrating that they do have an actual income need – and the income must be taken from the trust (usually monthly or annually and fixed for life) – and secondly, as this is a gift, on the condition that the settlor does not access the gifted capital in their lifetime. The client's ability to demonstrate their income need is vital. For example, one of my clients recently sold a holiday home for £400,000, which had been rented out for £20,000 per annum prior to the sale. By selling the property, the client then had £20,000 less income. I recommended a series of loan and DGP trusts; it was easy to demonstrate the income need to ratify the DGP discount as the client had a glaringly obvious extra income need as he no longer had the £20,000 holiday home income.

The DGP is an excellent IHT mitigation tool for a client who wants and can demonstrate a fixed income need for life, but who is prepared to forego access to the capital gifted, so any recommendation must be carefully tailored to the client's circumstances.

Gift trust

Quite simply, this operates in the same way as the DGP but with no income option or upfront IHT discount savings. The advantage to using a gift trust, as well as the trust protection as described earlier, is that the settlor can gift out trust capital both during the seven-year survival period and thereafter during their lifetime as the date of the gift into trust starts the seven-year survival clock.

A gift trust can also be enhanced by linking it to a whole of life plan. Effectively, income is taken on a monthly or annual basis from the gift trust in order to pay for the whole of life cover, which pays the client's IHT bill. This can be an excellent advice solution for the right client's circumstances and one insurance company in particular specialises in this scheme.

Whole of life cover

I always say that my "clever" clients will take out whole of life cover to mitigate their IHT liability. When your health is good, the monthly or annual guaranteed premiums payable after full medical underwriting are,

I find, an incredibly good financial deal and they offer an immediate IHT mitigation solution without having to survive the seven years for outright gifts to individuals or trusts (or two years with the BPR solutions).

Broadly, let's say you have an IHT liability of £250,000 and are married. In this case, a joint life, second death, whole of life assurance plan written in trust for £250,000 will pay out into the trust when the second person dies, and the IHT bill is therefore provided for immediately. It is possible to index both the guaranteed premium and benefit by inflation or a flat rate of one to five per cent, which is advantageous when, of course, the value of your estate is growing.

I recommend to my clients that the plan be set up in discretionary trust. This is vital so that, in this example, the £250,000 is outside of the clients' estate (and also outside of probate so that speed of payment is fast). In this example, the settlors of the trust would be the married couple, and they will appoint trustees, usually their children who are also the trust beneficiaries. I recommend also drawing up a "letter of wishes", which sits alongside the trust – this will typically direct the trustees to use the trust proceeds to meet the IHT bill and to divide any surpluses equally amongst the beneficiaries. Although this letter of wishes is not legally binding on the trustees, it gives them a clear steer as to how the settlors (their parents) want to have the trust administered, so in practice these instructions are carefully adhered to.

The great thing with whole of life cover is that, once you are medically underwritten and have been offered the monthly or annual premium from the life assurance company and the plan is therefore "in force" or "on risk", all you need to do is pay the premiums. Whatever sum assured you have chosen, this life cover amount cannot be taken away or the terms changed, even if your health deteriorates, as the premiums and benefit are guaranteed at the outset. What I often recommend to my clients is that they ask their children to pay some or all of the premiums, and why not? They are the ones who will benefit; however, to date I have not yet seen any of those children paying these plan premiums – instead the "bank of mum and dad" continues to cover them!

The beauty of whole of life cover is that, once it is in place, it immediately solves the problem of your beneficiaries having to pay the inheritance tax bill before they can access your estate.

Even if you don't bother with trust planning, outright gifts to your beneficiaries, BPR solutions or will arrangements, the simple fact is that if you have sufficient whole of life cover to meet your IHT bill, your inheritance tax problem is solved. Concerned about your estate growing? Simply index the plan premiums and benefit and you are inflation-proofed too. This is why I say that my "clever clients" will have taken out a whole of life plan for their IHT bill, and if you do so while in good health I find that the premiums are incredibly competitive.

A whole of life plan in action: a real-life client example

I have a male client, aged 60, and his wife, aged 52, who are both non-smokers and in good health.

£588,000 of cover is required to meet their IHT bill on second death.

Their annual guaranteed premium is £9,352.13 (this premium is guaranteed never to increase once they are medically underwritten and the plan is accepted and in force, no matter what happens to their health in future).

Let's do the maths: £588,000 of cover/£9,352.13 per annum premium = a "break even point" of 62.87 years.

This means that only after paying their premium for 62.87 years will the clients be paying more into the plan than the benefit they will receive. As long as the second death occurs no more than 62 years from the contract start date, this is a good financial deal for the client. Of course, in the meantime, the clients are fully covered for the £588,000.

The question I ask then is: "What is the likelihood you will both live longer than another 62 years?"

Mr would be aged 122 years and Mrs, 114 years – yes, medical science is improving but, come on, will we be living this long?

Solving the IHT problem – a typical but hypothetical client example

Let's return to **Ken and Carole**

Remember Ken and Carole, who I talked about earlier in the chapter? As a reminder, they are a couple near retirement age who have an IHT problem. Let's take a look at a potential solution to their IHT problem using the trusts and plans I've just outlined.

First, here's a reminder of Ken and Carole's problem. They have a joint estate of £1.85 million, which is made up of the following:

- Property: £650,000
- Investments (ISAs, VCTs, shares): £350,000
- Cash held: £650,000
- Personal assets: £200,000
- Total estate: £1,85 million

£1.85 million - £1 million (in IHT nil rate bands) = £850,000 x 40 per cent = £340,000 payable on second death

Let's also assume the clients require, over and above their pension incomes, an additional £8,000 net income per annum in order to meet their normal expenditure. Let's also assume that a part of their overall income would meet the cost of a joint life second death whole of life plan (see following example) to help mitigate their IHT liability in full.

As things stand, without taking any action to mitigate their IHT bill, Ken and Carole's estate would currently owe £340,000 in IHT that is payable on second death. However, there are several ways they can reduce this liability.

Using possible investments/gifts from cash assets, Ken and Carole could do the following:

*   Set up a Discounted Gift Trust for Ken for £100,000. This will remove £100,000 from Ken's estate (with four per cent income fixed for life after year one = £4,000pa) and deliver an upfront IHT discount, PLUS the full amount falls outside the estate assuming a seven-year survival for him.

- Set up a Discounted Gift Trust for Carole for £100,000. This will remove £100,000 from Carole's estate (with four per cent income fixed for life after year one = £4,000pa) and deliver an upfront IHT discount, PLUS the full amount falls outside the estate assuming a seven-year survival for her.

- Give a joint gift to their son of £50,000 (this will fall outside their estate assuming a seven-year survival).

- Give a joint gift to their daughter of £50,000 (this will fall outside their estate assuming a seven-year survival).

- Take out an IHT joint BPR product solution for £100,000 (this will fall outside of the estate assuming a two-year survival of one of the couple only).

In taking these steps, Ken and Carole have removed £400,000 from their estate, effectively reducing it to £1.45 million, assuming they meet the relevant survivorship rules. The £8,000pa from the two DGPs will also provide the top-up income they require, which is fixed for their lives.

Therefore, IHT payable assuming a seven-year survival: £450,000 taxable x 40 per cent = £180,000

Ken and Carole can then cover that final £180,000 with a joint life second death whole of life plan for £180,000. The premiums for this plan can be paid annually from their overall income OR, of course, their children could be asked to pay as they are the beneficiaries. The overall result of this advice?

IHT payable (assuming joint survival in line with the example given) = NIL

Ken and Carole could also consider a gift inter-vivos plan as described previously for the seven years before these gifts are outside of their joint estates.

Advice in action: G and R

My work with G and R

G and R are the son and daughter-in-law of two of my valued clients, who have been clients of mine for many years. G's parents have taken my advice over the years and we have taken steps to mitigate their IHT bill, as well as to diversify their overall investment portfolio and focus on all elements of their financial wellbeing.

In 2010, G's parents gave a substantial gift to him and his brother (K). Both G and K then became my clients and I invested these cash gifts for both of them. Over the years, G and R have continued to save into ISAs from their employment income and, in 2015 when R's parents sadly passed away, I advised them on further lump-sum investments.

In around 2019, G's retirement plans came to fruition; he was due a redundancy package and to take his DB pension, which had been fully funded.

In view of their investment experience and the income flexibility options with the DC pension route over the DB route, G and R were very keen to explore G's pension transfer options from his DB scheme to a DC alternative. This was despite my usual warnings surrounding "giving up" the valuable guarantees associated with the DB route.

We had a number of meetings to consider the transfer options and we provided cash flow analysis to help with the decision, together with forecasted returns of their current investments, R's pension and their state pension forecasts. We also took their detailed future monthly expenditure requirements into account.

The next step was to analyse their AFRO (age that their funds would run out) to ensure they would be comfortable longer term, given reasonable portfolio growth rates (and also building in potential investment market crashes) and taking into account all their assets versus their longer-term expenditure requirements.

In early 2020, G and R decided to transfer G's pension to a DC arrangement after this comprehensive due diligence work had been completed and they had fully reflected. Since then, we have met regularly and advice has been given to take an element of tax-free cash and income up to G's personal income tax allowance (so that he has not paid any income tax yet enjoys the income required from his now-DC pension) to meet their monthly expenditure requirements.

In future, meetings will take place at least annually and a full holistic review, as well as G's pension decumulation advice, will continue longer term.

In addition, financial reviews have been offered to their two children who are now in their 20s and may benefit from holistic inter-generational advice, so all three generations of the family can hopefully be helped with their financial planning longer term.

G's perspective

"We have benefited from Howard's help and advice now for over ten years, during which time he has advised us on regular, one-off and pension investments. He has also engaged with my parents, my brother and us to discuss inheritance tax planning and intergenerational financial planning.

I trust him implicitly to listen to our investment requirements and recommend a suitable investment product to suit our risk profile and growth expectations.

A great example of this is the transfer of my DB pension fund to a more flexible and usable flexi-drawdown arrangement.

I first approached Howard for his opinions on the appropriateness of undertaking a transfer in 2018 and was unsurprised that his initial reaction was one of scepticism, citing all the usual pitfalls regarding loss of guaranteed benefits etc. Several meetings followed during which it became apparent that, with respect to our current and prospective future financial position, a more flexible arrangement would better suit our requirements.

Over the course of several months and a succession of meetings, Howard and his team provided estimates, projections and options for potential pension investment/income drawdown strategies and, after completing due diligence with the SJP team, we concluded the transfer in June 2020. We have had a number of reviews since putting the plan in place, and I am very happy with the ongoing help and support of Howard and his team.

It is important to trust and to learn from the advice given by your financial adviser and it is Howard's integrity and ability to explain complex financial, tax and pension scenarios in understandable language that has allowed me to develop a better understanding of the value of financial planning. It is sometimes difficult to address emotional issues like inheritance tax, financial gifts and intergenerational planning, but Howard's empathetic approach and the trust that has been built up over a number of years have enabled us to address these issues as a family, and I hope in due course my children will also benefit from the same quality of advice.

Finally, it is important to note that while Howard is the 'face and voice' that is seen and heard, his team are equally important to delivering a quality, professional service."

Summary

With the right advice, trusts don't have to be complicated and you don't have to be afraid of them. They
are a very useful tool for mitigating IHT and keeping
money very much within your family, potentially
spanning generations. TIBs are a simplistic, flexible
and tax-efficient way to access capital and income
when required and, in the longer term, with the
right advice and service, pass the monies easily to
your beneficiaries.

The skill of the financial planner when dealing with
trust and estate planning solutions is to fully understand the client's IHT problem, how important it is for
them to have some or all of the bill mitigated and also
in what timeframe. It is vital that a blend of the correct
trust and BPR solutions is recommended, taking into
account the client's future capital access requirements and income needs as well as ideally engaging
the client's trustees and beneficiaries so that they also
understand the client's financial plan – all in liaison with
either an estate planning solicitor or STEP-qualified
planner where the client's circumstances require it.

Chapter 5:

Pensions & Investments

"Getting older is no problem. You just have to live long enough."

– Groucho Marx

Pensions are the most tax-efficient way of building a retirement fund, whether you are employed, self-employed or run your own limited company.

The need for us to take individual responsibility for our own retirement fund has never been greater and therefore the requirement for strong levels of advice, service and pension fund performance has equally never been so great. Gone are the days when, as a school or university leaver and in taking your first new job, you would stay with your first employer throughout your whole working life. In fact, it is more typical now for us to have periods of both employed and self-employed work and often a career directional change or two.

In this chapter I am going to focus on state, employer and private pensions largely; however, it is important to mention that there are a variety of assets that can form part of your retirement fund, namely:

- Residential buy-to-let property

- Directly owned business commercial property

- The future sale of your business

- Future lump sum inheritances and parental/relations' gifts/legacies

- Annual ISA usage and savings into other investments e.g. VCT/EIS/investment trusts/cash accounts trusts

- Investment bonds

- Trust funds

- Miscellaneous investments

VCTs are tax-efficient, UK closed-end collective scheme investment companies designed to provide venture capital for small and expanding companies. To encourage investment into these companies, the UK government offers some generous tax benefits, including a potential 30 per cent income tax relief on the amount invested and tax-free dividends. However, care is required in their selection and monitoring and, due to their higher risk nature, VCTs should only be considered where a client has already maximised their annual pension and ISA allowances. The investment amount should be matched to the client's appetite for investment risk and they should only be used as part of an overall balanced portfolio.

The EIS is a series of UK tax reliefs launched in 1994 in succession to the Business Expansion Scheme (BES). Significant tax breaks are available to investors across all three taxes – income, capital gains and inheritance tax. My view here is that an EIS investment carries a greater risk than a VCT and the importance of specific and tailored financial advice becomes vital given their complexity on all aspects, including their longer-term tax reclaim administration position. The same caveats as regards risk, investment amount etc (as detailed in Chapter 2 under golden rule number four) apply equally to EIS and to VCT investments.

Some of the previously mentioned assets can involve prior planning, such as building a property portfolio and building your business for a future sale, whereas we cannot be certain of when or how much we will inherit or indeed if we will receive gifts from those closest to us.

Certainly, our most income tax-efficient option is funding and planning through a private or employer pension scheme or plan and, whereas the previously mentioned assets will always be taken into account as part of a robust retirement fund, I want to concentrate here on employer and private pension funding.

Why is it important to have a retirement fund?

I think that I will live to age 95. My rationale is that my Dad, who had arguably a far less healthy lifestyle than myself, lived an active life to age 90 (he was a heavy industry manual worker and smoked cigarettes until he was aged around 60). So, with a little bit of lady luck on my side, I would hope that I would be kicking about into my mid-90s – I don't smoke, I don't drink that much alcohol, I exercise regularly, I hydrate fairly well and for the most part I eat a balanced diet.

Let's say that I retire fully at age 65 and I live to age 95 – that's 30 years of retirement funding I need where I am no longer earning a salary or a self-employed income. Let's do some broad sums – maybe I would like £30,000 net income per annum when I retire; how much will my pension fund need to be?

Again, these are very broad indicative calculations, but if I had £1 million in a pension fund, which was invested across a balanced portfolio of assets (pension, property, ISA investments etc), then, assuming a five per cent growth rate, I could take a £50,000 net income yield from that £1 million fund – but I want to be more conservative than that as I only require £30,000 AND I want my £1 million pension fund to pass onto my wife and two sons, thereby keeping pace with inflation. Therefore, hypothetically, taking a three per cent net yield (£30,000) from the five per cent yielding/growing portfolio will allow a two per cent broad hedge against inflation.

Whenever I am looking at broad cash flow modelling for a client, I like to assume a maximum income yield of up to four per cent (and no more) from their overall pension and investment portfolio. Four per cent is a good benchmark figure as, if their underlying invested assets are performing at, say, six per cent, there is an inflation hedge against the overall pension assets held.

If, therefore, your goal is to achieve overall pension assets of £1 million so that you can retire on a £30,000 or £40,000 net pension, the secret is to invest wisely and regularly and to start early enough to benefit from compound interest. Engaging professional help can be useful through regular, at least annual, check-in meetings, and using a cash flow modelling tool can help project your target amount of fund required (and therefore the regular amount you need to contribute) aligned to acknowledgement and valuation of the assets other than your pension plan (ISA, property portfolio, etc) which form part of your overall fund.

Building a retirement fund is important to many people so that they can achieve financial independence – the ability to choose when and whether they wish to work. Everyone has a different financial independence figure or "golden number". In the pre-retirement or accumulation phase of your life, the role of the financial planner is to find out your target number and to help you get there in the most tax-efficient manner possible. Number one in terms of tax efficiency is employer or private pension planning.

One of the important benefits of engaging a financial planner is the regular, ongoing service review or checkpoint meetings, which should be held at least annually to track progress across a number of key areas:

- Are your original retirement goals and
  plans still in line with our first meeting?

- Any changes to salary/earnings/health/marital status/career plans? Any inheritances/windfalls or bonuses/share scheme plans we need to consider?

- Do your pension funds require rebalancing? Rebalancing is returning the pension fund makeup back to the original asset class split so that your fund portfolio investment risk does not become skewed and therefore unbalanced.

- Does the existing pension plan still fit your needs, including the contribution levels and affordability?

- Should we consider ISA and/or VCT/EIS investments to boost your fund in the most tax-efficient manner in line with regular or lump sum funding?

- Has your attitude to investment risk changed at all since our last meeting?

- Should we carry out a further cash flow modelling exercise to ensure your long-term retirement goal age and projections are in line?

What are our retirement funding options?

UK State Pension

Whether you are employed or self-employed, you will currently qualify for a UK State Pension, depending upon your record of National Insurance Contributions (NICs). The easiest thing to do here, without me trotting out the varieties of state sension (SERPs/S2P etc) and their intricacies, is for you to obtain your own unique HMRC "State Pension forecast". All you need to do is to visit www.gov.uk with a form of identification (passport/ driving licence) and have your National Insurance Number handy. This 10-minute or so process will give you the current anticipated future date you will take your state pension and the projected weekly amount. If you are behind on your current NIC payments, you can make these up to ensure you qualify fully. This is a valuable forecast document to help build your longer-term financial plan as we will be covering in Chapter 8.

Employer pensions

There are typically two main types of employer retire-ment schemes offered: defined benefit (DB) (also known as final salary) and defined contribution (DC) pensions.

Nowadays in the private sector, DB pensions are almost a thing of the past and most private sector DB schemes are closed to new members in favour of their DC alternative. This is due to the huge and ongoing balance sheet liability and maintenance cost to the employer associated with a DB scheme. Public sector schemes for our NHS, teachers and civil servants, for example, continue to offer DB schemes as a valuable and well-deserved retirement benefit to our public servants.

Put simply, DB pensions are superb – not only does the guaranteed income benefit escalate in deferment (if you leave the scheme early) but they also escalate upwards automatically each year in payment when you take them, in line with statutory escalation which is already built into your pension from the time and service you have built up. With a DB pension, all of the risk and the requirement to pay the accrued benefit to the employee is with the employer; the employee has no risk or need to maintain/manage or make investment decisions surrounding a DB pension at all; and the employee only has to pay a percentage of their salary (unless it is a non-contributory DB scheme, which are very rare these days), which is usually deducted from their pay on a monthly basis. They can simply sit back and enjoy the monthly indexed benefits at the scheme retirement age. Because of these valuable guaranteed DB benefits, any transfers away from private sector DB schemes to a DC alternative (public sector schemes cannot be transferred) can only be advised once thorough client due diligence has been undertaken and the client fully accepts the risks and fees involved.

DC pensions are the main type of employer scheme currently offered because of the ever-increasing balance sheet cost of their DB alternative described previously. This means the employer and employee contribution (or amount invested) is defined, but the benefit, in polar opposite to the DB scheme, is definitely not guaranteed. This makes life easier and more cost-effective for the employer – instead of having an unknown but contractual DB liability in future and the DB scheme management responsibility, once the DC employer payment (usually a fixed percentage of the employee's salary) has been made, the performance risk is with the fund managers appointed within the DC scheme.

Questions I will always ask a new client are: "Where are your current DC pension funds invested? Which provider are they with, who are the fund managers and in what asset classes are the funds invested? What special or guaranteed protections, if any, do they have in place and what are the funds' current and transfer fund values? How have these funds performed in the past, who gives you advice and service on these funds, sets contributions and projects their future benefits in line with your retirement goals and who will give you advice on an ongoing basis, especially when you want to access the fund benefits?"

Once I have the answers to these questions I can then formulate an objective and professional recommendation as to whether these plans should be either retained with their current providers or transferred to my firm. Comprehensive due diligence is required before any pension transfer is recommended. Over the years, many clients have benefited from this holistic advice approach and consolidated some or all of their pensions in order to achieve better long-term and ongoing advice, service and performance.

An auto-enrolment employer pension scheme, run by providers such as NEST and the People's Pension, is a DC pension introduced by the government in 2012. It is an excellent idea first mooted by the Labour government to bridge the "pensions gap" so that all employees would have access to their own individual DC pension fund as well as any state pension available to them when they become eligible. Previously the 1999 "stakeholder pension" legislation did not force the employer or employee to contribute and, as a result, did not have widespread take up and therefore largely failed.

Other types of pension scheme

Prior to 2006 and the "pensions simplification" legislation, there were many forms and types of pension. If you have an older scheme, pre-2006, it may come with valuable protected tax-free cash (above the standard 25 per cent) or guaranteed annuity payment rates – advice to both understand these schemes and how they fit into your holistic requirements becomes important.

SIPPs and SSASs

The Self Invested Pension Scheme (SIPP) is a pension whereby the client can make their own investment decisions and choices and invest in a wide variety of asset classes, most notably directly into commercial property (but not residential property). A SIPP holder also has the ability to borrow money against the plan value – typically up to a maximum of 50 per cent of the plan value. SIPPs can be an excellent retirement funding choice and can offer many tax benefits. My view is to take financial advice before you take one out. Over the years, I have seen many clients who own one but do not use it for its intended purpose and instead would have been better off with an often less-expensive, standard DC personal pension/retirement account.

Trustee pension investments can be added to a SIPP and, in my experience, work particularly well; this is also true with the SSAS as described in the next paragraph, the SSAS being a type of small occupational pension scheme.

A Small Self Administered Pension Scheme (SSAS)

These schemes are trust based and are suited to groups of individuals who run common businesses and wish to have complete control of the pension fund. Unlike a SIPP, an SSAS can lend capital as well as borrow. There is no requirement for a trustee professional to be appointed; however, SSAS rules are complex and may well prove difficult for clients without experience of running a scheme pension. Again, before establishing an SSAS my view is to understand the purpose of doing so and the more complicated longer-term management of the scheme.

Death benefit differences – DB and DC schemes

DB schemes

With most DB schemes, on death of the member when a DB scheme pension is in payment, a 50 per cent spouse's benefit (or a person who can demonstrate a financial dependency) is payable for life, which will escalate in payment. Children are only covered up to the age of 23.

DC schemes

The death benefits on DC pensions are stronger than their DB alternatives as a general rule. If a DC policy-holder or DC scheme pension member dies pre-age 75, then 100 per cent of the DC fund value is paid out. Post-age 75, beneficiaries can either buy an annuity, continue a drawdown pension themselves or take the whole fund in cash minus a hefty tax charge.

Because of these death benefit differentials between DB and DC schemes, where a client is in poor health and is divorced, single or has children over the age of 23, in certain circumstances and after the necessary due diligence, it may be advantageous for that client to transfer their DB pension to a DC arrangement to take advantage of the better death and succession benefits. Again, thorough, detailed and researched advice surrounding the client's circumstances and the risks involved must be carried out, including cash flow modelling to establish the client's expenditure requirements in retirement versus the projected requirements so that the age that their overall pension and investment funds may run out (AFRO) is clear. An overriding responsibility for the financial adviser is to ensure their client never "runs out of money".

The accumulation stage – pre-retirement

With the current pension lifetime allowance (the amount above which, when benefits are taken, there is an additional tax charge) set at £1,073,100 and frozen until 2026, the school or university leaver still has plenty of scope to maximise their employer's DC pension or, if they are very lucky, DB pension. The lifetime allowance has been on a steady decline from a generous £1.8 million in 2011, with staged jumps down to £1.5 million, £1.25 million then to £1 million before indexation increases to the current level (now, however, the current level is frozen until April 2026).

Do not delay starting

£3,600 gross (£2,880 net of upfront 20 per cent tax relief is the amount you pay) can be added annually to a DC pension regardless of age or earnings, so starting a plan for your children or grandchildren can be incredibly good for their retirement plans. My view here is that if you start one for your children/grandchildren, review it regularly, make the contributions worthwhile for them and ideally add the maximum £3,600 gross per annum each year. This will give them a significant start as a young adult when they start earning their own money and indeed continue contributing to the plan themselves – advice required, of course, depending on their circumstances.

Within our industry, there is much talk about the negative impact of the "cost of delay" in regard to pension planning. Because of the effect of compounding returns, a delay in starting your pension will have a dramatic effect on the returns achieved at the point of you needing them.

Not many people can claim to understand compound interest, yet we all recognise its effect when we see it.

Compound interest works in the same way as compound growth.

The pension rules are very clear about one thing: we have a choice of how much we contribute and when. To put it another way, we have a choice of what we can do in retirement and when our retirement can start. The key decision is when we start to make worthwhile investments. The sooner we start, the more choices we have later.

If a level gross investment of £10,000 per annum to a registered pension scheme commenced at age 30, subject to the assumptions shown in the following table, a projected fund of £463,000 would be available at age 60. This example shows what could happen if the start of the regular annual contribution was delayed by five, ten or 15 years.

	Fund Value	Reduction in Fund	% Reduction in Fund	Increase in Annual Contribution Needed to Provide a Fund of £463,000
Five-year delay	£358,000	£105,000	23%	£2,919 pa
Ten-year delay	£266,000	£197,000	43%	£7,360 pa
15-year delay	£186,000	£277,000	60%	£14,848 pa

The benefit of pound cost averaging

This is where, when we add long-term monthly or annual regular contributions to our pension, we receive an "averaging" benefit as, when markets are high, our monthly contribution buys fewer units in our pension fund, but conversely when markets fall, our monthly contribution will buy more units – often, however, when markets fall my clients become gloomy. However, I ask them to remember that when markets fall they should actually "cheer" as their monthly investment is actually buying more units in their pension plan. I then ask: "When will you be needing the pension money?" This is often many years away, so those cheaply acquired pension plan units on the back of a market fall have a long time to grow and recover. Even if a client is nearing retirement, the likelihood is that these monies will later enter income drawdown so will still be longer-term invested and have time to recover.

Upfront income tax relief

Pensions are the best vehicle for saving for retirement because of the upfront tax relief available. The current pension annual allowance is £40,000, on which it is possible to "carry forward" the previous three tax years of unused allowances and obtain tax relief at your highest marginal rate of income tax provided your earnings support the contribution. Advice here on the calculation becomes important.

For example, if you are a higher rate taxpayer, a £100 contribution to your DC pension will cost you just £60 as an employee or if you are self-employed. You pay an upfront contribution of £80 net of 20 per cent basic rate tax, and your pension provider claims the other £20 back directly on your behalf from HMRC. Then, via your annual tax return, you make a claim for the other £20 (20 per cent) so that you have received the full £40 back and therefore 40 per cent tax relief on your £100 contribution.

The income tax relief position improves even further when a client earns more than £100,000. For every £2 this client earns over £100,000, they see their personal income tax allowance drop by £1 so that, in tax year 2021/22 when their personal allowance is £12,570, if they earn more than £125,140 they lose this allowance completely. By adding a personal contribution to their pension, they can claw some or even all of this personal allowance back. In the example of the £125,140 earner, a gross pension contribution of £25,140 would cost them just £10,056 net after the reliefs are applied. The saving differential of £15,084 gives an effective tax relief rate of 60 per cent (£15,084/£25,140 = 60 per cent).

Salary sacrifice and pension contribution limits

Salary sacrifice schemes can be advantageous for both the employer and employee. As an employee, a salary sacrifice scheme allows you to "sacrifice" some of your salary and have that paid directly into your pension fund. For example, if you are earning £55,000 a year, you could choose to "sacrifice" £10,000 of your salary. This means your pay would drop to £45,000 gross for income tax and NICs purposes, with the £10,000 "sacrifice" amount being paid directly into your pension as an employer contribution.

This £10,000 doesn't "touch" your topline on your payslip and it brings a number of benefits to you beyond the contribution to your pension. Firstly, in the example just given, it brings your salary down below £50,070 a year, which is the threshold for paying the higher rate of 40 per cent tax on your earnings in 2021/22, saving income tax at 20 per cent. Secondly, it will also reduce your employee NICs commensurately.

A negotiation point with an employer here is to have their savings (13.80 per cent) of employer NICs paid to your pension instead of to HMRC, as they would have paid HMRC on your £10,000 sacrificed contribution if you had kept your salary at £55,000. My starting point conversation on behalf of my client to their employer is: "Why not redirect this NIC saving for them, please? Your valued employee will benefit instead of HMRC and the net cost to you is exactly the same." Sometimes it works, sometimes it doesn't – usually because the employer cannot be bothered with the administration burden.

Asset preservation trusts (APTs)

The APT can also be termed an "interspousal bypass" trust. They are used for company death in service benefit or, more commonly, for DC pension plan death benefit tax protection, and are particularly beneficial should the plan owner die before age 75. In the example of a DC pension scheme, the settlor of the APT, which is a discretionary trust, is the plan holder, who will nominate trustees (usually close family/friends) to become legal owners of the potential trust capital (death benefit – when the client passes away). Legally, the trustees must act in the best interests of the beneficiaries (usually a spouse as a potential beneficiary and children as default beneficiaries). Importantly, if the client (settlor) dies before the age of 75 the tax-free death benefit, if it is then added to the APT, will fall outside of the spouse/survivor's IHT estate and therefore outside of their estate on second death for IHT purposes.

The APT cash trust proceeds, safely outside of the spouse's estate for IHT, are available for income/capital as required and a proportion will typically be invested. The settlor/client can write alongside the APT a "letter of wishes" which, although not legally binding on the trustees, gives the trustees guidance on how the settlor would like to have the trust proceeds administered, distributed and invested.

The decumulation stage – taking your retirement benefits

So, you have taken advice, paid into your pension, saved tax along the way and you now, at retirement age, want to enjoy your hard-earned wealth and income and have a long, happy and stress-free retirement. While I believe annual ongoing financial advice, service and performance is important in the accumulation stage, I think it is absolutely vital in the decumulation or "at retirement" phase.

ISA

An Individual Savings Account (ISA) is an "umbrella" – it is NOT a fund or a direct investment itself. This "umbrella", however, is extremely valuable as it completely shields the underlying capital invested (currently £20,000) from both income tax and, arguably more importantly, capital gains tax. We can add cash, direct equities or investment funds into this tax-free umbrella. With the ability of a basic or higher rate taxpayer, however, to receive £1,000 or £500 per annum respectively from gross paying cash accounts then the argument for holding cash within the ISA umbrella becomes severely weakened.

Where service and advice become particularly important with ISAs is when a married or registered civil partnership client sadly dies. The ISA umbrella, since 2018 under something called an additional permitted subscription (APS), can be passed from the deceased spouse to the surviving spouse via probate so that the tax-efficient ISA umbrella is not lost and the survivor retains it.

It is also possible, again with the right advice, to "auto-ISA" a lump-sum, longer-term investment. This is where a client invests cash capital in line with the seven golden rules, after having considered their most tax-efficient option, which is their pension maximisation – a larger lump sum than their annual ISA allowance (£20,000 in the 2021/22 tax year). Remember, an ISA is just a tax-efficient "umbrella". What you can put under it is largely cash, direct equities or unit-linked funds. The auto-ISA works such that if, for example, a client had £100,000 cash to invest and the annual ISA allowance remains at £20,000 for the next five tax years, £20,000 is automatically transferred just after 6 April from the £100,000 unit trust fund and put under the ISA umbrella each year for five tax years so that the whole amount is then covered under it.

This advice can be particularly valuable longer term for the client who then has a large amount invested in ISAs. Should they wish to liquidate their capital in full or partially, not only is there no income tax but more importantly there is also no CGT, which could be significant had the monies been left exclusively within the unit trust (as the whole gain on surrender would be chargeable to CGT). I recall a married couple who had over £500,000 invested in ISAs and wanted full and immediate access to buy a second property. The ISA monies were repaid just before their second-home completion via a call to our office and a written instruction. This repayment was made not only at no exit penalty but also with no need for the client to inform HMRC of any chargeable gains for CGT as the ISA umbrella shielded the gain position.

In November 2011, HMRC extended the ISA umbrella allowance to those under the age of 18 and the "Junior ISA" was born. In the 2021/22 tax year, a minor can add up to £9,000 and this valuable additional ISA allowance can help the whole family's intergenerational holistic financial plan.

Lifetime ISAs were also introduced in April 2017. An excellent consideration for those over age 18, up to £4,000 per annum can be added with the government adding a 25 per cent bonus when buying a first home or saving for later life. The £4,000 lifetime ISA limit is within the £20,000 overall ISA allowance, not in addition to it. This ISA can be an excellent choice for the young person wanting a boost, particularly to their first home purchase deposit, and I like it.

DB Pension – lump sum and income options at retirement

All DB scheme pensions will offer a defined benefit income on retirement, which will increase annually in line with statutory escalation based upon the scheme accrual rate (typically 1/60th), the length of the member's service and the level of final salary at date of leaving (unless it is a Career Average Scheme; then it is, of course, based upon your career average earnings). DB schemes also offer a tax-free lump-sum payment in addition to the pension income, payable by what is known as "commutation".

Commutation is defined as giving up part or all of the pension payable in exchange for an immediate lump sum. Commutation factors (calculated by the DB scheme actuary and typically 12/1 or 15/1, for example – meaning that for every £1 of income given up £12 or £15 of lump sum is made available) are used to determine the amount of pension which needs to be given up in order to provide the lump sum. Therefore, at retirement it is common for members to be offered the choice of taking their pension in full or, as an alternative, an immediate tax-free cash lump sum and a lower residual pension (which allows the pension given up to provide the cash).

This is where advice becomes so important, and clients will often use my knowledge and experience as their "sounding board" on the various options available in line with their income and lump-sum objectives. Once your DB lump sum and income options have been chosen they cannot be changed, so it is important we get it right.

DC pensions – lump sum and income options at retirement

Whereas a DB pension is designed to be taken at the scheme normal retirement age (it can be taken earlier if the scheme allows it, but not before age 55 unless via ill health), often 60 or 65, DC schemes can be accessed currently at age 55 (which will increase to age 57 in April 2028).

The first income option is to buy a guaranteed income, known as an annuity. This can be written as single life, which means upon your death the pension dies with you. Or it can be written as joint life where it can be protected on your death, usually with 50 per cent or 100 per cent of the benefit going to your spouse or civil partner. In order to keep pace with inflation, the annuity can be bought to escalate in payment either on a flat fixed percentage rate or in line with RPI or CPI.

The annuity option is a first port of call for any DC pension decumulation advice as it is guaranteed, simplistic and requires no further advice or maintenance (unlike income drawdown). For the inexperienced investor, who does not want or need to take any risk with their pension pot, the annuity route can be a sensible one and MUST always be considered by the financial adviser.

Despite the underlying annuity guarantees, many clients aren't keen on them, especially right now when annuity rates are very low for a variety of reasons. Instead, many clients prefer the flexibility of access and better death benefits available via income drawdown.

Once again, this is where professional advice becomes so important. The annuity option, even when a client enters income drawdown, should never be closed and always be re-visited at annual financial servicing reviews. This may become important to consider for a client who in future has a health setback where an impaired life annuity will offer the chance of a greater guaranteed income due to their limited life expectancy.

Income drawdown is the other way of drawing a DC pension and, as I've said, it is often the favoured route for many of my clients at present. Let's say that you have a £1 million DC pension fund. At retirement age, the standard 25 per cent of the £1 million fund can typically be taken as a tax-free lump sum. The remaining £750,000 could be used to buy an annuity or it can enter income drawdown (it is possible to have a mix, which is especially important when a client wishes to guarantee an amount of their pension income via the annuity and then requires the flexibility that income drawdown affords).

Phased retirement option with income drawdown

You do not have to take all of your DC pension fund tax-free cash in one go (and this can also be applied to annuities).

Let's come back to the £1 million pension fund.

You are newly retired, it is April 2021, you do not intend to earn again and, aged say 60, you require for the first year only (as your income need will be appraised annually at our annual advice review meetings) a tax-efficient income of around £3,000 per month. One easy way to do this could be to crystallise (by which I mean release tax-free cash from) just ten per cent – that is £100,000 – of your £1 million fund. The other £900,000 remains as a pension (it still has its tax-free cash availability intact for future years).

£100,000 x 25 per cent = £25,000 tax-free cash divided by 12 months = £2,083 per month paid to you – maybe you can put this into your savings account and set up a standing order to pay £2,083 of your tax-free capital to your current account to help to meet your required total £3,000 per month expenditure.

The £75,000 left after the £25,000 tax-free cash has been taken moves into income drawdown where you take an immediate monthly withdrawal up to your personal income tax allowance (£12,570 in 2021/22 tax year).

£12,570 divided by 12 = £1,047.50 per month paid to you with no income tax as it is within your band allowance.

£2,083 tax-free income plus £1,047.50 non-taxable income = £3,130.50, exceeding your required monthly income need of around £3,000. You're living life as a NON-TAXPAYER!!!

In 2022, as part of our annual review of your pension and your income options, this exercise would be repeated and, of course, with £900,000 still in the pension, in theory this client could do a similar thing for the next nine tax years (which assumes no growth – very unlikely) and enjoy income that is completely income tax free before their pension was all completely added into income drawdown. This advice and service can continue to offer an income tailored to your circumstances, with the annuity option always open (health problem or guaranteed income required). Also, of course, pension legislation will very likely change across the years – your financial adviser needs to be "on the ball" to these changes to amend and change advice for you as it occurs. This is again why local service and advice from a firm you can trust becomes vital.

Advice in action: C and G

My work with C and G

C attended my investment seminar in 2016 and I first reviewed their financial circumstances a few days later at their home when I then met G. The couple were aged in their early to mid-50s with two grown-up sons who were financially independent. They had no debts and were comfortable with their life cover protections via a policy they held, as well as company death in service benefits.

C, a local government officer, had a public sector final salary pension scheme with over 27 years' service and G had a mixture of DB and defined contribution pension schemes. He was employed as a national sales manager for an engineering firm, which meant he travelled during the week extensively.

They held substantial investments in bank and building society savings cash accounts. Their initial goals were to fully retire at around age 60. In October 2018, G took a job closer to home and in November 2019, aged 58, fully retired, taking his DB pension lump sums and income in early 2020.

C continues to work part-time; however, she has plans to retire fully in early 2022.

My advice has centred around ensuring they utilise their respective investment ISA allowances over the years since 2016, so that their cash savings reserves beat inflation in the longer term via carefully chosen and explained medium-risk diversified fund port-folios. Previously, the clients had been fully invested solely in cash accounts.

G's DB lump sums have been invested similarly, but we have been careful to ensure the clients have always had sufficient cash reserves for short-term emergency needs.

C's attitude to investment risk was more cautious than G's and this was reflected therefore in a more conservative portfolio choice for her. We also consolidated G's DC pension plans in 2017 in a similar diversified fund fashion to ensure future advice, service and performance can be given easily on them.

I recommended the services of a STEP-qualified will writer to ensure their wills were professionally drafted, which they acted upon. They had already made LPAs.

In 2021, at our annual review of their circumstances and investments, their portfolios had performed at 7.2 per cent net and 4.2 per cent net respectively – G's slightly more adventurous medium portfolio performing, as would be expected, better than C's more balanced one.

Also in 2021, in line with G's full retirement and in anticipation of C's, the clients are to take an income of £500 per month from each of their ISAs commencing early 2022, which will match their monthly income needs. This will be reviewed again later in 2022.

Finally, the clients' two sons have been contacted for financial reviews by my colleague who is looking to help them initially with mortgage and pension advice.

<u>G's perspective</u>

"It was quite clear from C's enthusiasm with regards to Howard's Financial Seminar and our subsequent meeting at home that his professionalism, integrity and enthusiasm gave us the confidence that we were entering into a long-term financial relationship.

We both feel that Howard's financial planning advice and assistance has enabled us to retire earlier than expected and feel extremely financially secure for our retirement and continuing in the lifestyle we are accustomed to.

His advice, support and assistance have been exemplary and we would have no objections to recommending him for financial planning in the future.

Howard is always available at any time for advice/questions and very prompt at responding to our requests. His administration staff are extremely helpful and courteous and complement his services extremely well – a great team and we thank Howard and his team for their help over the years. We look forward to continuing our partnership and exceptional investment performance, which we are extremely happy with, in the coming years."

Summary

In the 30-plus years I've been working in this industry, I have seen major changes to pensions. Further changes are inevitable, which is why it's so important to take ongoing advice from a chartered pensions specialist. Their ability to react swiftly to legislation changes, to explain them to you in layperson's terms and to incorporate them into your ongoing annual financial plan is invaluable.

There are a number of your other assets and investments, as well as your pension plans, that need to be taken into account in establishing an overall retirement fund valuation, and the benefit of a cash flow modelling meeting is that it can give you the motivation and peace of mind that your saving plans are on track.

Advice, service and performance are equally important in both the pre- and post-retirement stages of your planning journey, so hiring a firm and adviser who will follow through in these areas long term is important – not just on plan establishment.

Start early and plan at the outset. You should also review, at least annually, your overall retirement plan. A good retirement financial planner and firm will tailor this plan for you and work with you to set up a SMART individual retirement plan, stretching your ability to save tax efficiently and yet affordably. They will also motivate you along the way to achieve your desired result, which can often be financial independence, and then help you enjoy the fruits of the plan for the remainder of your life.

Chapter 6:

Later Life Advice

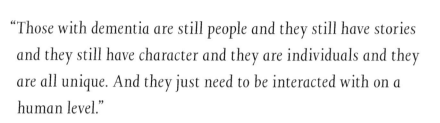

"Those with dementia are still people and they still have stories and they still have character and they are individuals and they are all unique. And they just need to be interacted with on a human level."

– Carey Mulligan[8]

8 Adam Brimelow, (2012), 'Carey Mulligan supports bid to raise dementia awareness', BBC, 21 May, available at: https://www.bbc.com/news/health-18115205

The topic of later life advice can be a subject that some of us want to avoid, but aside from the financial impact of not planning properly for your later years, there is the emotional impact this can have on your loved ones. When it comes to later life advice, there are several important elements to consider beyond the financial.

If we look at an average person's general happiness, if they have good family/friends and social opportunities close by, take regular walks and exercise well, eat a healthy and balanced diet and have no financial worries then most people will consider themselves to be "happy". As we get older, social opportunities with close friends become fewer and fewer, we will at some point sadly lose our life partner and it can be more difficult to exercise and prepare balanced meals due to increasing infirmity, so the last thing we need is to have any financial worries.

I believe there are four pillars for the elderly client that the adviser must consider in relation to their holistic needs to ensure they are able to live as full, happy and independent a life as possible, for as long as possible. The first of these is **sociability**. What kinds of interactions does your elderly parent or relative have with friends and family? Are they sociable? Are they lonely?

There is a significant issue with loneliness in the UK and this is particularly prevalent among the older generation. Dementia is one of the main long-term health conditions that is likely to affect us as we get older, but you have to ask whether a lack of socialisation as we get older makes dementia become even more pronounced.

The second pillar is **exercise and physical health**. How is your parent's physical health? Do they have access to places for nearby walks, or even gym facilities? Can they exercise at home? The third is **nutrition**. What we eat and how we fuel our bodies is very important throughout our lives, but especially as we get older. Are they getting all the nutrients they need in their diet? Is their alcohol consumption steady? The final pillar is **financial stability**. Are they on a strong financial footing and financially comfortable so that they do not have to worry about money?

As an accredited SOLLA adviser, I will take all four of these pillars into account when I am providing advice around matters related to later life in advising the elderly client (or typically advising their attorney under an LPA on their behalf). My role in this position is to support not only my client but also their family because they will often be the ones who have to support my client as they age and potentially make important decisions on their behalf.

This journey can be emotionally challenging for the attorneys, often the children, who are having to balance doing what they can to support the elderly person as they become more physically and/or mentally infirm as they age with their own lives. It can be very difficult to juggle your own life with looking after a parent, especially if you do not live close by.

What counts as later life advice?

Later life advice typically covers the stage when you need care or assistance, which can either be provided at home or in a residential care or a nursing home. Although it is easy to think of "later life" as being applicable to people in their 80s and 90s, the reality is that you could be diagnosed with a condition such as dementia in your 40s or 50s, in which case this kind of advice will be equally relevant.

Fundamentally, what I consider and review for my clients is that they are not only financially self-sufficient but that, as they age, their overall wellbeing and ability to live happily and independently is continually reviewed, with their family consulted and supported whenever I have concerns. There are four general progressions when it comes to care needs, starting with help at home, which could be employing a cleaner, home additions such as personal alarms in the event of a fall, key box home entry to allow medical help, engaging the local authority for "meals on wheels" or asking a social worker to visit for socialisation support. From there, the next step could be sheltered accommodation (for example, a retirement apartment with community socialisation support and even medical help). As we get older and require more one-to-one support, a residential care home could be the next step, and then full-time nursing care in a residential nursing home may be required.

While we all need to consider these four pillars when considering our later life care, many clients come to me because they are concerned about the financial implications of needing long-term care and that is definitely where most advisers' focus is directed.

The picture of long-term care in England

As we all know, in the UK the government, especially post-Covid-19, has a horrendous amount of public debt. When it comes to social care, the fact is the government simply doesn't have the money to fund all of our long-term care needs, which means that some or all of this expense can fall upon us as individuals.

In 2021, Rishi Sunak, the UK chancellor, proposed a 1.25 per cent NIC tax hike badged as a "health and social care levy" which, among other aspects, will be designed to limit the amount we have to pay towards our long-term and social care with an outline 2023 implementation date. We have been here before, however. Back in July 2011, Andrew Dilnot produced a 400-plus page coalition government-backed dossier for a reformed social care system, some elements of which were acted upon within the Care Act 2014. What is yet to be implemented, however, was his proposal for a lifetime care cap between £35,000 and £50,000. Broadly, UK-wide, if we require paid care either at home or in residential care, we will be asked to contribute unless we have next to no assets. If we do have severe medical needs, then we may qualify for authority funded Continuing Health Care or Funded Nursing Care.

There are certain state benefits we can claim, such as attendance allowance and carer's allowance.

It is the later life adviser's responsibility to navigate the client and their family through the full local authority financial assessment process, showing them the state allowances available and signposting other organisations that can help such as Age UK and Dementia Friends. They will then work out a financial planning solution to meet the cost of the care individually tailored to the client's position and, importantly, ensure that this planning solution is then regularly reviewed.

It is worth acknowledging that we are very lucky with the level of NHS and local authority care support we receive in the UK. No one is left destitute; the NHS is there for any acute emergency medical need and if you truly cannot afford later life care, your local authority will provide it for you.

There are many places in this world where people do not receive this level of support, such as America. I remember chatting to a taxi driver in San Francisco on a visit there in 2014, and he told me that a lot of people in his limited financial position, with little medical health cover, hope for a "quick kill", so that they don't have a long, drawn-out illness and rack up substantial long-term care medical bills that will be left for their families to pay. That was a real eye-opener for me and so I believe we should acknowledge how lucky we are to have our NHS and other local authority support systems in place.

Domiciliary care

Domiciliary, or at-home, care is usually the first progression when it comes to later life care. Engaging with your local authority is very important at this stage because there are certain things available, such as personal alarms, that can help you to live in your home independently for longer. They will also put together a care plan to support you at home in liaison with a local social worker support person.

A personal alarm is simply a badge/button/dongle you wear at all times, so that if you have a fall at home, you can press the button and a call will be put into local paramedics to request assistance and to inform your loved ones. The local authority can also help with your home security by installing keypad access to your home so your family and, if needed, paramedics/emergency services can gain access if you need urgent help, for example, if you have a fall. As a SOLLA adviser, I will signpost my clients to organisations like Age UK and the local authority, who can help to put these things in place. Age UK can also help the family with things like how to claim attendance and carer's allowance benefits. I might also signpost a person living with dementia and their family to a local "Dementia Friends information about dementia course", which can help educate family members and anyone supporting a person who is living with dementia on how best to understand and support them.

I might also recommend that the family consider bringing in a cleaner/gardener or engaging a home help person to help them prepare food or with simple socialisation. Age UK can have a volunteer visit their home as part of their "befriending" programme, which offers the elderly client much-needed social support. This is a journey that many families will go on, and it is one that I have been on myself with my Dad.

Howard's story

As I mentioned earlier, I am an only child, so when my Dad started to need support on the four pillars mentioned previously, I went on this journey with him. In his later years, after having survived three heart attacks and a minor stroke in his early 70s, my Dad had always had a very healthy and balanced diet. In the winter, each week he would usually make a batch of vegetable broth, which would be his lunch for the week, and he knew how to cook his favourite meals for tea. In the summer, he would switch instead to eating salads. However, in his late 80s when his dementia became more pronounced, one early summer's morning he rang me up and asked: "Howard, how do I make the salads again?" I realised he needed real day-to-day help.

At this point I engaged a lovely local lady who would visit him a few times each week and remind him how to make his food, help him make it, keep it both tasty and healthy and make sure that he was safe while he was cooking and preparing it. She helped him with socialisation too and he enjoyed her company. She also helped keep him active; she would take him on local walks and trips out in her car as he had to give up his own licence due to his health. Basically, she helped and encouraged my Dad to live independently for as long as possible.

I also organised for a cleaner to go to my Dad's house regularly. All of this meant that he was also having regular social interaction with different people and, of course, I would visit him regularly too and we would look forward to watching Sunderland AFC play at home (if you can call that enjoyment!). We also got him a personal alarm through the local authority. Financially, he was in a strong position. All four of those pillars were being met and he was able to stay in his home. The recommendation is always to try and help someone continue to live happily and independently at home for as long as they are able to while meeting all four pillars.

In March 2018, and I remember this day very well, I received a call from the paramedics to say that my Dad had suffered a fall at home. It was Saturday morning when I got the call: he'd fallen, pressed his alarm and the paramedics had reached him via the keypad access we had had fitted. He was frightened following the fall and he was admitted to hospital. Thankfully he hadn't seriously hurt himself, but this was when I realised that a decision about his future care needed to be made. It wasn't safe for him to be left at home on his own.

I had LPA, as we discussed in Chapter 3, and I knew that after this Dad couldn't go back home and endure more time on his own because there was a risk he could fall again and that next time it could be more serious. A quick decision was needed on where his needs would be best taken care of after he was discharged from hospital.

My Dad had a property, cash assets and investments, so he was self-funding his care. Because I knew this, and this is one of the advantages of self-funding, I was able (with the help of my wife Gill who went along with me) to look at two or three dementia care homes in the Sunderland area to find the right one for him. Within a week of being discharged from hospital, he had moved into a ground-floor room in a local dementia care home. He settled fairly well and at least I knew he was safe throughout the day and night. I took one day off from work each week in 2018 to visit him. We would go to the local park and he would sing his Frank Sinatra songs there and back in the car. We would have a coffee in the park and he would love to see families and dogs running around enjoying themselves. His illness became progressively worse; it was a tough time.

Although I was able to visit him regularly and knew that he was being well looked after, it is incredibly difficult to watch a loved one living with dementia because you witness first-hand the effect of the illness on them – I would liken it to getting your "guts ripped out" every time you visit. Many years before, I went on a Dementia Friends course as part of my SOLLA training, so I understood the basics of the disease's effects and how it progresses, but it was still very difficult to see it happening in my own Dad.

From the financial side, I looked at how best to fund Dad's care. He only had a basic state pension, so I applied for the attendance allowance state benefit on his behalf. I applied for this twice on his journey; the first time I applied was while he was still living at home and it was refused, but the second time it was granted. Attendance allowance is only around £90 per week, so it's not particularly generous but it is non-taxable.

With the attendance allowance and his state pension benefits, my Dad had an income of about £1,000 per month. The cost of care, when he was admitted to the dementia care home in March 2018, was around £3,000 per month, which meant he had a shortfall of about £2,000 per month that needed to be found.

I had several options to fund this shortfall in my Dad's case. The first one I looked at is called an immediate needs annuity. I will explain what this is in greater detail later in the chapter, but in my Dad's case it would have required an upfront payment to an insurance company of £60,000 in exchange for the monthly shortfall of £2,000 per month to meet his care needs for the rest of his life. I decided against this option at the time, the reason being that my Dad had capital invested, and I felt that a better option would be for him to take an income yield from this capital to meet the shortfall instead of going down the annuity route.

Therefore I used his property and affairs LPA to commence a £2,000 per month income yield from his investments to make up the care home bill shortfall, and I organised and paid for the monthly care invoice payment on my Dad's behalf.

As it turned out, my Dad passed away in December 2018, aged 90, nine months after having been admitted from hospital directly to the care home I had chosen for him. Financially, which by the way was the least of my worries for Dad, the net cost to his estate for his care was £2,000 per month for the nine months he was there, so a total of only £18,000. Had I instead taken the immediate needs annuity route for him, I would have paid out £60,000, which would have been a bad financial decision (although I could have opted for some short-term annuity capital protection, which I more than likely would have done). Of course, had my Dad lived for another ten years then that £60,000 annuity investment would have been a very good one, paying out around £240,000 – so it is always worthy of consideration.

The reason I have shared this with you is to show you that I understand the journey you may have to go on when you are making decisions about your loved one's wellbeing and financial affairs, having been there myself.

The importance of LPA

I explained the purpose of having an LPA in Chapter 3, but hopefully now you can see why it is so important to have this kind of document in place well before you need it. Without an LPA, you will have to apply for deputyship with the Office of the Public Guardian, an office within the Court of Protection, and this process can take months, which you obviously don't have when you are making decisions about the immediate care and wellbeing needs of your loved one.

I had the property and affairs LPA for my Dad, as well as the personal welfare LPA. I used the former on several occasions to make the necessary financial arrangements to provide for my Dad's care, but, just before he passed away in December 2018, he became ill and went into hospital. In the final week of his life, decisions had to be made around sustaining medical treatment. I was able to make those decisions, with the excellent support of the doctors, under the powers vested in me by the personal welfare LPA.

Solutions for funding long-term care

Clients often come to me and tell me that they are worried about how they might pay for long-term care for themselves, or for themselves and their partner if they are married. If you are also concerned about this, there are a few things you can do.

Pension income

Start by looking at your total income across your state pension, private and DB pensions and indeed any other sources of rental income etc. Often your pension income can be quite large. You can then compare your annual pension income to the cost of residential and/or nursing care in your area. In many cases, my clients tell me that the cost of residential and/or nursing care in the North East of England (where I am based) is around £35,000 to £45,000 a year, but if their pension income is enough to meet the bill then there is no need to worry because they have sufficient guaranteed pension income to pay for their care, probably for the rest of their lives, especially where their pensions escalate upwards in line with inflation.

In addition to this, where you do not have sufficient pension income to meet your care needs but do have investments then, as in my Dad's position, an investment income yield can be organised from the investments to help meet the shortfall.

Using your property

Another potential solution to funding care costs if you go into a residential or nursing home is to rent out your property. The yield from renting your main residence could fill any gap between the cost of your care and your pension income. This will also mean that your home doesn't need to be sold immediately.

It is important to highlight that, if you are married or in a registered civil partnership, your main residence is disregarded for the local authority long-term care financial assessment where your spouse/partner is still alive and therefore still living in the property. Only after first death, therefore, is the property taken into account for the financial assessment purposes in this case.

You could also explore releasing equity from your property. If you are considering going down this route, I strongly advise you to do your research about the equity release firms available to ensure you choose a reputable firm. One of the things you should look for is a firm that is SHIP (safe home income plan) registered.

Local authorities also offer a type of equity release scheme themselves, through what is known as a deferred payment plan. The local authority takes a first legal charge on your home, using the notional equity (plus an interest rate charge) to set against your care bill charges. When you pass away, the property is sold, the local authority takes their share of the care charges plus interest to date under their first legal charge and the remainder is distributed to your estate under the terms of your will.

Income from investments

If you have investments, you can take a similar approach to what I did with my Dad and take an income yield (I always favour a maximum yield of four per cent as I covered in the pensions chapter) from those investments to make up any shortfall.

Immediate needs annuity

As I mentioned in my story about my Dad, one of the options when you're self-funding your care is an immediate needs annuity. This is where an insurance company will offer you an annuity (a guaranteed, fixed or indexed monthly payment paid tax free for life and paid directly to the care home/provider, designed to be sufficient to cover the difference between the annuitant's total current income and the cost of care in the residential/nursing home) in exchange for a lump-sum, one-off payment.

These annuity plans are individually medically under-written, so when you apply for one the insurance company will look at the person's medical history and make an assessment about how long they are likely to live before giving you a quote for the lump sum they require in exchange for the chosen monthly annuity payment to the care home.

As I said, in my Dad's case he had a care bill shortfall of £2,000 a month and the insurance company's indi-vidually medically underwritten lump sum guaranteed annuity offer to him to provide the £2,000 per month fixed for the rest of his life in the summer of 2018, just as he was turning 90, was £60,000. In my Dad's case, this would not have been cost-effective as he died just five months later. However, for some clients, to protect the annuitant's estate against longevity risk, this can be a good financial option for complete security that your loved one's care is secured and guaranteed for life.

The annuity can also be indexed so that it goes up each year in line with increasing care costs. It is also possible to take out a deferred annuity (the payment to the care home kicks in after a one, two or three year period) and both short- and long-term capital protection options can be incorporated into the annuity quote. The skill, time and patience of the later life adviser becomes important here to the client and their family so that all parties fully understand all the options available before making their decision.

Later Life Planning Scheme

This works in a similar way to the discretionary trust solutions I have covered in Chapter 4. An investment bond is placed into trust for say £50,000. Upon seven years' survival, the whole amount is outside of the settlor's estate for IHT. The client can also nominate a contingent income – the contingency is IF they require long-term care then an income stream can be taken from the trust. So, in tandem with IHT mitigation advice, this can provide a long-term care income solution for the right client's circumstances.

The deprivation of assets rule

The reality is that you don't have to be wealthy to pay for your later life care and, in fact, a great many people will have to self-fund their care costs. I sometimes meet people who tell me that they are going to transfer ownership of their home to their children so that it won't make up part of the financial assessment if they need long-term care.

As I mentioned in Chapter 3, you have to be very careful if you do this. Firstly, if the local authority finds that you have only transferred ownership or put your property into trust to avoid paying for your care, they can call it back into your estate and it will still form part of the assessment under the "deliberate deprivation of assets" rule. If you do transfer ownership of your property to your children, unless you pay them a fair market rent (as they are the property owners), then you are open to a local authority deliberate deprivation rule plea.

Also, remember that you will have given the property away. What happens if the family falls out? Not a pretty picture, being evicted from your own home by an estranged son or daughter-in-law – do you need this kind of stress?

If you are considering either an ownership change or adding your main residence to trust to avoid potential long-term care fees, I would urge you to think very carefully and seek legal advice before doing so. You have to make sure you fully understand the deliberate deprivation of assets rules and that any trust or scheme will not fall foul of it when challenged.

As I mentioned earlier in this chapter, you also have to consider that if you rely on your local authority to pay for your care, your options over where you or your loved ones are cared for are likely to be much more limited.

The importance of later life advice

Whatever option you are exploring to fund your long-term care, it is really important to take advice from an experienced, and ideally SOLLA-qualified, financial planner. This advice is important not only from a financial perspective but also an emotional perspective. I can help you consider all the options not only financially but also from the point of view of the other three pillars I mentioned at the start of this chapter, namely, the social aspect, your (or your loved one's) nutrition and physical health and exercise needs.

As I mentioned, the first step for many people as they get older is to introduce domiciliary care at home. When that is no longer enough, there is a step in between this and residential or nursing care, which is sheltered accommodation or a retirement village. These can be a great middle ground because they provide a social element, there are typically facilities on site to support your physical health and mobility and there are people who can support you with your nutrition. You're safe and secure, but can continue to live a relatively independent life. If your children or immediate family don't live close by, this can be a good option to give all of you peace of mind.

Albert's decision

Albert was living in a bungalow but his health started to deteriorate and he realised he couldn't continue to live at home. His close family lived down in the South and he did not want to be a burden for them. He was diagnosed with cancer and took the decision to buy a retirement apartment in a development run in his local town by the Joseph Rowntree Foundation.

As well as providing him with his own apartment, where he had his own ground-floor space so that he could relax and live independently, with direct access to a communal garden, he had onsite medical care 24/7, a swimming pool, gym, cafe and restaurant. Regular social events were also organised, so he was able to meet other people and make friends, while exercising as much as he was able to and being confident that his medical needs could be taken care of. The onsite restaurant provided balanced and healthy meals so he had the option of using it when he did not want to cook for himself.

I say very well done to Albert for choosing to take up, on his own initiative, his long-term care needs himself, and I applaud the Joseph Rowntree Foundation for setting up such excellent local facilities. I remember visiting Albert at this place many times before he sadly passed away. He was able to enjoy his later years in a comfortable and safe environment where the four main pillars of socialisation, nutrition, exercise and finance were all under control for him.

I sincerely hope that here in the UK we have more places like the Joseph Rowntree Foundation available to us in the future – perhaps it is the responsibility of all of us to lobby the politicians and council leaders to ensure that we have better care facilities available nationwide?

Cultural differences in later life care

I have talked about the various options for later life care, including retirement villages (Joseph Rowntree Foundation), residential care homes and nursing homes, but in some cultures it is much more common for children to look after their parents as they age and, in doing so, they avoid many of the financial costs associated with long-term care, as well as ensuring that their parents have regular social contact with the family.

This attitude towards care is particularly prevalent in Indian and other Asian communities in my experience, and in my view it is to be commended. If you can support your loved one as they age and look after all of the four pillars for them, then what a fantastic legacy you leave to your family rather than allowing others to manage their care needs.

Of course, every family is different and what is possible for one will not be possible for another, but I would hope there is a nationwide cultural shift so that more of us can care for our elderly relatives. This would take the burden away somewhat from the local authority and surely would promote healthier and happier overall family lives?

The importance of financial education

The earlier you can start to think about later life care, the better. One of the issues I repeatedly hear about is the belief that it is better to keep your money as cash than it is to invest it. As we know from the golden rules of investing in Chapter 2, this isn't the case because inflation will erode its value over time.

One of the reasons why so many people still have this false belief, however, is due to a lack of financial education, which is something I would like to change. Not everyone is in a position to seek financial advice, but I believe that basic financial education could help people make much better decisions around their money, both now and in the future. Personally, I have a short-term goal to visit my old local schools and help them with financial education. This is an initiative that my firm supports and the plan is to deliver basic learning sessions around financial topics, ranging from why it is important to save, the value of money and the basics of tax to how stock markets work and how to save and apply for a mortgage. By providing early education and motivation for our young people and the next generation around financial matters, perhaps we can help more people to have financially secure futures?

Summary

Considering our later life care is something that all of us are going to face as we get older, and it isn't always easy. However, with good advice and service, this is a journey that can be shared and navigated as happily as possible for both you and your family.

Forward planning is essential, and considering your options early, as well as making sure you have important documents such as an LPA in place, will make that journey smoother for all involved.

Taking advice from a SOLLA-qualified financial planner can make the financial and emotional journey for both you and your family happier and smoother too. You don't have to do everything on your own and, particularly when it comes to later life care, the decisions that have to be made are about considerably more than just money, as I have discussed in this chapter. You also have to consider your socialisation, nutrition and physical health when you are making decisions and planning for your future. This is why I would strongly recommend that you seek out a financial planner with a SOLLA qualification, rather than simply going to an IFA who does not have experience in this area.

Chapter 7:

Other Investment Options

"I will tell you how to become rich. Close the doors. Be fearful when others are greedy. Be greedy when others are fearful."

— Warren Buffett

I'm not going to cover all the investment options available to you because there are too many to mention in one book, let alone one chapter. Also, some of the investments I cover here were covered (or at least received a mention) when I talked about diversification within the seven golden rules I outlined in Chapter 2. What I am going to talk about, however, are some of the most common enquiries I receive from my clients, to give you an idea of some of the many investment options out there.

I also want to start this chapter by being very clear: these are not areas in which I advise and recommend products or services. While my clients often come to me asking for advice about these kinds of investments, my response is always the same: "I can give you some generic information and I can read their marketing brochures for you and replay some of the features, but I cannot give you any specific advice as to whether or not you should invest – the final choice must be your own so please, before committing a penny, do your own due diligence." What I will do, however, is ask a few questions back to them to test their knowledge on the investment and also to seek to ensure they understand why they are investing.

Fancy a wee dram?

Ben phoned me, and emailed me a marketing brochure, to ask my opinion on an investment opportunity and I could tell he was excited about it. "I've sent you some information about whisky, and I'm thinking of putting £10,000 in. What do you think?"

I said: "This isn't an area that I advise on, but we can have a chat." My first question, regardless of the investment, is always: "Do you understand it fully?" and I put this to Ben.

I suggested he consider the accessibility of the investment, his £10,000, as well as the fact that he'd be making his life a little more complicated by adding another investment to his portfolio. I asked about whether he enjoys whisky himself and about the risk associated with the investment price fluctuation longer term. I also asked if the investment was regulated by the FCA.

We talked around the potential downsides to the investment for a short while and then I said: "Why are you so keen to invest in whisky?" In this case, one of the reasons Ben was attracted to the investment was because he had a passion for whisky himself. He wanted to learn more about the distilling process and felt he'd really enjoy dabbling in this area.

At the end of our conversation, I told him that it was entirely his decision whether or not to invest, but also that he should think carefully about how much he wanted to put in initially and not to "put his shirt on it", i.e. to go all-in and potentially open himself up to significant losses that would affect his financial situation and lifestyle.

The outcome? Ben invested. £10,000 was just a small part of his overall investment portfolio, he could afford to lose it all, he has a passion for whisky, saw the opportunity and felt he could not only make some money but also that he would enjoy the ownership ride – the right outcome all round.

The scenario I just shared there is not uncommon. I often have clients contacting me to ask my opinion on an investment opportunity that has come their way. As I said in Chapter 2, if something sounds too good to be true then often it is, and it is important that, whether you're thinking of investing in whisky, a classic car, a racehorse or anything else, you apply the seven golden rules of investing. But sometimes, if you follow your heart and your passion, so long as you do not invest too much and understand the pitfalls, life is too short – so "just do it".

One of the biggest things to look out for with any investment is whether the underlying provider is FCA regulated, as the regulation can afford valuable safety guarantees.

Let's run through some of the most common "miscel-laneous" investment options that I have come across over my years in the industry and I'll give you some of the outcomes and stories along the way – the purpose here is that you may avoid the bad ones and under-stand the potential risks before you invest in that "next best thing" offer which will no doubt come your way.

Peer-to-peer lending

Peer-to-peer (P2P) lending is the practice of lending money to individuals or businesses through online services that match lenders with borrowers, cutting out the financial institution as the intermediary. The company that maintains the online platform charges a fee for both borrowers and investors for the provided services so that they maintain a profit margin and a reason for trading.

Advantages can include:

- Higher possible returns to investors – because of cutting out the intermediary perhaps?

- A more accessible source of funding with lower interest rates charged for some borrowers than conventional lending – often due to the poor credit rating of the borrower or non-standard loan type; therefore the investor picks up this additional risk.

Disadvantages can include:

- Credit risk: borrowers applying to a P2P lender may have been refused a loan from a conventional lender – the investor is in effect picking up this risk.

- Regulation: although P2P lending has been regulated by the FCA since 2014, clients need to understand the additional risks of default given the extra lending risk.

When investments go sour

Judy invested around £200,000 into a number of P2P lending schemes/products before I was introduced to her as a client. She diversified her money across six or seven different P2P lenders, but one of those schemes, with around £25,000 of her capital invested, announced liquidity and bad debt problems after she had held it for a year or so. She has had the stress of trying to get back as much of her money as she can, along with the other people who invested in that same scheme.

In a recent update, she told me that she expects to get around 80 per cent of her initial £25,000 investment back, but this has been a hugely stressful and time-consuming experience. While this particular fund went very sour, it is worth noting that some of the other P2P schemes she invested in performed quite well compared to cash interest rates. However, whether this total investment was worth the time taken and stress overall is another question – a better alternative might have been a balanced portfolio of funds invested across the main asset classes, investing in real assets for the longer term.

Penny shares

Penny shares are shares in smaller growth companies that are trading at a very low price, that is, at around 1p in value. If that 1p share grows in value quickly, and let's say it shoots to 2p, then you sell out and, of course, double your money – sounds great, doesn't it? However, if that company goes bust, you can lose everything you have put in – not so great.

Penny shares are, again, not an area I advise upon; I am not a stockbroker. However, if you are interested in having a go at investing in them, I would simply say be cautious and don't put all of your money into them. A famous printed magazine, The Penny Shares Guide, sent to subscribers every two months seeks to highlight shares worth 50p or less and pick the growth "winners" from the "losers". Many years ago I subscribed; it does have very good analysis and information and I did like their system of "stop loss", where the reader is encouraged to set a "must-sell" price IF their penny share reaches either their benchmark high or low price. This system is designed so that gains are taken and losses can never be too painful, e.g. I buy at 20p and if the price rises to 30p I sell and bank my 10p gain. However, if the price drops to 15p, I nurse the 5p loss but at least I do not walk away with nothing and have limited my downside.

Share clubs

Alternatively, you can get together with others to form your own local online or face-to-face "share slub". Share clubs or investment clubs offer a fun way to invest in the stock market without the investor having to put down a large investment amount. Maybe a group of six or more like-minded equity/share investors will invest perhaps £50 to £100 per month into their share club bank account. At each monthly meeting, every member will, in turn, have the opportunity to "pitch" their best share pick from their own research. The group votes and that month's "kitty" is invested in the share, which is added onto the investment list for the next meeting's monthly review (whether then to sell/hold or buy more). As well as the social side, share clubs offer a good way to have fun in being your very own share fund manager and, with the right selections and a good "stop loss" system as covered previously, maybe a little profit will also come your way.

Responsible investing

Financial returns matter, but so does the impact our investments have on society and the environment. The impact our choices have on society and the environment has never been greater: everything we do, from the food we eat to the types of products we buy and the way we travel, has a consequence for the world around us. It's no longer acceptable to invest in businesses for profit alone, when those with poor practices can have such a profoundly negative impact on the world around us. Quite simply, the investment decisions we take today define the future for us all. As I write this, the 26th Conference of the Parties (COP26) has just finished in Glasgow, making us all acutely aware that we can "no longer use our planet as a toilet", that mere words are no longer enough and that the whole world must be united to remedy the effects of climate change.

It's my core belief that strong Environmental and Social Governance (ESG) principles – considerations relating to people, the planet and fair play – enhance and improve both investment returns and real-world outcomes. With a rising tide of people wanting their money to perform well, we, both as investors and as stewards of capital, need to take full responsibility for the change.

Socially responsible investing is about leaving a legacy, not just for your immediate family but for the planet. It focuses on a longer-term legacy of 50, 100 or even 200 years' time and ensuring what you are investing in now is good for our planet. Who wants to invest in something that's highly profitable but also highly damaging to the planet and the environment? This is why I would strongly recommend that if you are investing, you use a firm that has a very strong commitment to ESG and doesn't just pay lip service to it.

If this is something you are concerned about, and you want to ensure that all your investments are responsible, make sure you ask questions of your provider or financial adviser to find out where your money will be invested and how that fits into ESG. Dig a little deeper to make sure that their fund managers and investment houses aren't just ticking boxes or saying what you want to hear and that they are really fulfilling the purpose of an ESG investment, which is to do the right thing for people and the planet.

Responsible investing is not only about taking environmental and social responsibility; it also makes sound investment sense. By identifying financially material risks and opportunities relevant to the long-term sustainable growth of a company, we can not only protect our world but also secure the financial future of our clients who invest in these funds.

The firm I represent is committed to ESG from the top management down and throughout the organisation. All of our appointed fund managers are signatories of United Nations Principles for Responsible

Investment (UNPRI) and ESG meetings are regularly undertaken with our fund managers, consultants and data providers.

Depreciating assets

Depreciating assets are assets that can, and typically do, fall in value over time, such as cars, motorhomes, caravans and holiday lodges. Of course, there are exceptions: buy the right classic car, hold it long enough and it becomes more desirable for a potential strong gain, but for the most part these kinds of assets will depreciate in value.

Cars

For example, Trevor and his family have a BMW X5. They have owned it for ten years, it has over 100,000 miles and has been a reliable, relatively cheap and low-maintenance family car. It has depreciated gradually over the years, but all in all it has done the job for the family without it costing them a fortune.

Sarah and her family buy a brand new car every year. They buy their cars on finance deals that have high interest rates and the brands and models they buy depreciate quickly in value, so not only is the asset they buy depreciating quickly, but they are also paying out high finance costs for the privilege of owning them. Are they thinking more about "keeping up with the Joneses" rather than viewing their car as a vehicle to get them from "A" to "B"?

Where are you as regards car ownership? Like Trevor, like Sarah or somewhere in between? This all said, many people just love cars – you only have one life as I keep mentioning, so if you can afford it and love it then buy that Maserati, Bugatti, Aston Martin or Nissan!

Motorhomes

Clients often come to me, particularly around the time they retire, and tell me that they would like to buy a motorhome. These often cost between £50,000 and £100,000 so the first thing I always say is: "Make sure you use it!" You can go on a lot of holidays abroad for that kind of outlay, not to mention that the motorhome will need to be maintained and that the more miles it clocks up, the more its value will depreciate – but, again, if it is going to give you years of pleasure and memories then buy it!!!

Howard's story

I made my worst investment in 2009 when I bought a caravan holiday home at a holiday park in Weardale, 50 miles from my home in Sunderland. As a child, my family had a caravan near there in St. John's Chapel and I wanted to replicate those happy family times. We paid £25,000 for it, so not a huge outlay, but the annual holiday park maintenance fees started out at £2,700 and every year they would increase by around ten per cent. The pros were that the park was well-maintained, with a nice bar, lodge and children's play park, and if there was ever a maintenance problem with the caravan then the lodge owners would put it right very quickly.

The cons were that, every year, the site owners were very keen to have you upgrade (keeping up with the Joneses again) your caravan, either at an extra cash cost or on an expensive finance deal. As I've mentioned, the annual maintenance fees were high after the first year and became progressively more expensive. After two years, we said to ourselves "enough is enough" and looked to sell the caravan – the park owners offered us just £9,000 for our two-year-old £25,000 caravan and we had to take it or leave it as they would not allow an external sale. Now, we did enjoy the two years on the site and we had some lovely holidays, but boy oh boy did we pay for it!!!

By way of contrast, in 2016 we bought a small freehold holiday cottage, again in Weardale, in a remote village on the Cumbrian border called West Blackdene. The cottage backs onto the River Wear and you can hear the river running past our windows. The cottage has no garden, so it's easy to maintain. It's been a much better investment than that caravan – it cost us £110,000 (you can pay this for a caravan or holiday lodge now) and, by owning the freehold, if we do want to sell it in the future, we can. It has been not only a great investment (its value has increased sharply post- Covid-19 due to the UK's desire to holiday at home) but also a favourite holiday place for our family. Further, the maintenance costs (fuel/council tax etc) on an annual basis are still far less than we were paying ten years or so ago for the caravan park's annually increasing maintenance fees!

Timeshares

Timeshares are another investment that you need to go into with your eyes open. Much like my story with the caravan, these can depreciate considerably in value, have annual costs associated with them and be difficult to sell if you buy in the wrong location, which can impact upon the secondary sale market. Coming back to the golden rules of investing, you simply need to make sure you fully understand what you are putting your money into, how you can sell it on and what precisely the ongoing costs of ownership are – that all said, a timeshare can offer many benefits without the full responsibility of outright ownership.

Property abroad

Buying a property abroad is another investment people often want to make, but like with caravans, timeshares and motorhomes, this should be a very considered purchase. If you would like to buy somewhere abroad, be very careful about which country you buy in. Most EU countries have stable governments and economies and are only a short flight or, as is the case with France, a car journey away so the temptation to own and invest can be great.

Different jurisdictions have their own legislative and bureaucratic requirements, however, together with requirements for you to protect your own interests longer term. For example, if you own property abroad, say, for example, in France or Spain, you should have a will drafted in that country directing your interests, as your UK will is not sufficient. You should also make sure you understand the inheritance tax and succession laws, which can differ from those in the UK.

Think about what area you are buying your property in and whether it will be easy to sell should you decide to. I know many clients who have retired and chosen to live abroad for ten or 15 years and then decided that they would like to move back to the UK, often due to medical reasons and because they want access to the NHS. However, it can take time to sell their property overseas, which is why it's important to consider the second-hand market and how liquid that asset will be long term before you buy it (think – location, location, location).

Even if you aren't planning to move abroad, there will be costs to maintain the property when you aren't there, as well as expenses such as insurance and the money required to furnish it.

As a cautionary tale, I have one client who bought a property in a Bulgarian ski resort some years ago. Not only was the property three hours from the main airport, which made accessing it difficult, but the second-hand market in the area then plummeted, making it very difficult for him to sell it and he tells me it is almost worthless now.

Some of the questions I recommend answering before you buy a property abroad are:

- How much will you use it?

- What is the saleability like?

- Do you understand the laws around inheritance/ property ownership in the country you're buying in?

This is not to say you shouldn't buy property overseas. If you love a particular country or perhaps you're a builder and you would like to renovate a property in, say, rural France, or even if you just fancy it, then buy one. Remember, as I keep saying: "you only live once" and look at, for example, how strong my UK holiday home has been as an investment. When you have a good legal ownership title, buying overseas in a stable country with a desirable second-hand sale market can be a good investment as well as an excellent holiday home for precious family time.

I am not authorised or regulated to provide investment advice in this area, so I will always advise my clients to carry out their own due diligence within the country they intend to invest in before they commit.

Art

If you are an art lover, purchasing fine art can be an attractive investment and one that serves the dual purpose of being something that you will see and enjoy in your home every day. Art also doesn't attract capital gains tax or income tax, although it is still classed as part of your estate for inheritance tax purposes.

However, it is worth bearing in mind that the second-hand market for art can fluctuate, so if you need to sell your pieces and liquidate those assets, it isn't always easy to realise their full value.

Gold

Gold is another asset class that many people like to hold as part of a diversified portfolio, but as with any other investment the key is in understanding it and the risks involved. Where gold is concerned, you want to know where it is stored, how it is insured and which provider or merchant you are buying through, who, of course, needs to be reputable. The next time the stock market has a crash or a wobble watch out for the news highlighting that there has been a "flight to gold", meaning investors have ditched their shares in favour of tangibly owning gold bullion. This is all very well, but the question then comes around as to when you sell back the gold and go back into the stock market? I covered this under the golden rule of diversification earlier – if you hold a well-diversified portfolio, you will not need to worry or change investments as you will already own gold, either directly or indirectly through funds.

Remember that gold and precious metals will form part of a well-diversified, multi-asset alternative asset fund, which will typically be included within a balanced portfolio of investment funds. Therefore, through this type of fund you can invest indirectly, and perhaps more cheaply, in this asset class without having to manage and have the responsibility for the tangible and direct ownership of the gold.

Summary

All of these different assets – art, gold, property over-seas, whisky, motorhomes and caravans and so on – can be part of a diversified investment portfolio, but the key here is diversification. I am always very clear with my clients that these are not areas which I am authorised or regulated to advise upon. I will ask questions, like the ones I have shared in this chapter, to encourage each person to consider the investment from all angles, but ultimately it is down to them to carry out their own due diligence, involve an accountant, estate agent, solic-itor or other professional where it is necessary and/or seek alternative advice from someone who specialises in investments in that particular area.

Come back to the seven golden rules of investment before you make any investment decisions. Does what you're considering meet those rules I shared in Chapter 2?

Part 3:

What About You?

In this final part of the book, I am going to pull together everything we've talked about so far to explore how to create your financial plan and who can support you in this. Personally, I find creating financial plans for my clients one of the most rewarding parts of my job because most people want to know that they have enough money so that they'll never run out in retirement, and it is wonderful to give them that peace of mind and show them they have financial security.

For those clients who don't already have enough, a solid financial plan will show them exactly what they need to do and how much they need to save to get there. I use cash flow modelling software to track your journey from the accumulation stage, where you are building up your investments and pension, to the decumulation stage, where you are spending the wealth you have created during your lifetime. This software tracks not only the money that you are putting away but also the expected investment performance across your chosen investment portfolio in the future.

The reason that creating a financial plan is so rewarding for me and empowering for my clients is that it provides absolute clarity about your financial situation, both now and in the future, and it clearly demonstrates what you will need to do if you have specific financial goals around your retirement.

Strong financial planning will help you see the benefit of your investments and give you certainty that you are planning for a secure retirement and a financially secure future, not only for you but also for your loved ones who will potentially inherit from you. In the final chapters of the book, we will look at what goes into a comprehensive financial plan, as well as the importance of having a support network to help you not only to put a financial plan in place but to stick to it and realise your goals for your financial future.

Chapter 8:

Your Financial Plan

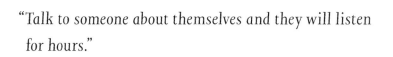

"Talk to someone about themselves and they will listen
for hours."

— Dale Carnegie[9]

9 Dale Carnegie, (2006), How to Win Friends and Influence People, Vermilion,
28th edition

In my experience, most people want to know that, if they're going to be saving money during their lifetime, they will never run out when they reach retirement. The amount you need to be financially independent is often referred to as your "golden" or "magic" number. This number will be different for everyone, but what I can tell you is that the earlier in your life you start thinking about this and get a financial plan in place, the more time you have to realise it and therefore the more likely you are to achieve it.

Why is a financial plan important?

Having a financial plan in place is important because it allows you to project forward and plan regular check-in points along the way to make sure that you are still on track for your retirement. Typically, clients want to achieve financial independence by the time they are considering retirement, but that doesn't mean they necessarily want to give up work if they enjoy it.

If this sounds like you, you could consider a phased or staggered retirement. This part of the plan ceases to be about money but instead is about ensuring you still have a fulfilling life after you retire or start to scale back your work. This might mean making sure you have hobbies and leisure interests. However, the biggest word to focus on is your "purpose" in life.

Making sure you have a clear purpose post-retirement is especially important if you are currently a busy professional, executive or entrepreneur because you have likely spent years and even decades striving to achieve your financial goals and looking after your clients. If you have a business or job you love, it can be very difficult to suddenly give that up, which is why it's essential to put a strategy for retirement in place that not only involves hobbies and activities but also a real purpose. For many of us, our purpose revolves around helping other people and our community, and being able to do this gives us great satisfaction in retirement.

Over the years, I have seen some clients who work until they are 60 or 65, retire and then find that they're bored. Some of them struggle so much that they even go back to work because they miss it so much.

Taking the time to think about your purpose once you retire is so important in my view because it may make your retirement more worthwhile and enjoyable. That said, many people may feel that they have done "their bit" for society via a 40-year career and may instead be blissfully content with family time, hobbies/interests and travel. I have seen a number of my clients, however, pursue and enjoy things such as working with a local charity, joining organisations such as the University of the Third Age (U3A)/Rotary or volunteering as a magistrate, which gives them the satisfaction of handing something back to their local community and keeping the grey matter working, as well as meeting new people socially.

Getting started with a financial plan

Cash flow modelling software, such as Voyant, is very useful for creating financial plans because it displays your information in a very clear format. The key to getting the most out of this software is ensuring the accuracy of the information that is input into it. Among the information that we will put into this software is your income, assets, ability to save surplus income and your expenditure, as well as potential windfalls such as an inheritance and potential life events like weddings, house moves etc.

The point of this stage in creating your financial plan is to get a very clear picture of where you are now and link that to where you want to be when you retire, let's say at 55, by planning and projecting the utilisation of your pensions, investments, ISAs and other assets to meet your objectives. Your financial plan will include details about the expenditure you want in retirement, including the likely step down in expenditure needs as we age – this can all be measured, projected and explained using the software.

Once you have got a financial plan in place, it is simply a case of executing the steps outlined in it and, from my perspective as a financial planner, having regular (at least annual) check-ins with my clients to make sure they are on track. I generally advise my clients to see me at least once a year so we can assess their progress.

Complex vs. simple financial plans

It is possible to put together your own simple financial plan with the information you have available to you about your pensionable assets and your current financial position. You can start by gathering all the details and projected values of your savings, investments and pension schemes. You can get a current statement of the benefits available at retirement within your DB scheme from the scheme trustees (to get an indicative capital value of a DB scheme, simply multiply the projected income in retirement figure by 16) and projected benefits from your DC schemes (this is simply the projected fund value at selected retirement age). If you have any buy-to-let properties you will know an estimated value/equity available. How complicated this plan is will depend on how many and what financial assets you have, but for most people this should be a relatively simple exercise.

For example:

DB scheme value: projected income of £20,000 × 16 = £320,000

DC scheme projected values: £280,000

Investments projected values: £200,000

Rental property equity: £200,000

Total fund = £1 million

I have already covered that a "reasonable" income yield to expect from a well-diversified portfolio is circa four per cent, so an indication of income expectation from the £1 million portfolio example, put simply, would be £40,000 per annum. This is a rough guide – it's better to complete a full cash flow modelling exercise – but some clients only want an estimation so using this method can work for them.

So, this can give you a valuable starting point for building a more comprehensive financial plan, and this is something you can do yourself.

However, I would recommend engaging with a financial planner who can use cash flow modelling software with you to develop a more complex and comprehensive financial plan. The information you input initially will be everything I've just talked about, but what your financial planner can do with this, along with an understanding of your income versus expenditure, is create a very detailed financial plan that you can adjust and review along the way.

Working with an adviser and using cash flow modelling software

Within this software, you can also build in different scenarios to see how certain events might alter your financial plans. As I have touched upon already, this can include the likes of a future inheritance, a child's wedding, business sales, gifts to your children, major holidays and so on. A good financial planner will ask detailed questions about your future plans beyond your assets alone during their fact finding meeting because this will allow them to create a base plan, as well as a number of future life changes and variations based around the different scenarios just described.

It is also important to note that your plan isn't fixed. If you were to create a financial plan at the age of 25, chances are that ten years later this is going to have changed substantially. This is why ongoing advice and annual reviews are so important because they allow your financial plan to evolve as you do, and this is also an opportunity for you and your financial adviser to grow together. Of course, your life goals will change over time, but if you point the ship in the right direction initially then you have a better chance of reaching your destination.

In fact, your relationship with your financial adviser is crucial to this process, and building a financial plan is a process. If you're going to knock a nail into the wall, you're not going to do it with a hammer in one hit – you tap away at it gradually. It's the same with a financial plan – initially set the outline plan then keep reviewing it annually just like that nail – tap, tap, tap until it is hammered home.

You and your financial adviser have to get to know and trust one another, and you want your adviser to ask the second, third and fourth questions to really get under the skin of what you are looking to achieve longer term so that the plan is tailored exactly to what you require.

Building a long-term relationship with your financial adviser

It is important to note that no one is indispensable and, even if you build a strong relationship with a particular adviser, it is also essential to ask about the firm's succession plan because your adviser won't be around forever. What you are looking for is a firm that has many capable advisers, any of whom can pick up your file and work with you if your current adviser is unavailable or has moved on or retired – a seamless transition to continue long-term service, advice and performance to yourself and your family. As a client, this gives you great peace of mind because you know that you and your financial future, as well as your next generation, will be in safe hands when your current adviser retires or has to leave the business for any other reason.

The key is that the other chartered financial planners in the business are not only suitably qualified but that they have similar personal qualities and values to your current financial planner as this will allow you to build an equally strong relationship with them.

If you are looking for a financial adviser, you should interview them before you decide to engage with them to make sure there is a right fit for you – not just a personality fit but, more importantly, what will future review meetings look like and does the firm have a robust succession plan in place? Some of the questions I would recommend you ask include: How many clients do you currently look after? What happens if you reach capacity and can no longer look after me? Who would see me then? Who will succeed you? After I have become a client, how often will you review my circumstances and what is the agenda of those meetings?

I'll give you an example that I've experienced, although not with a financial adviser but with a personal trainer. In 2013, I met a great personal trainer who was diligent, knowledgeable and who understood where I wanted to head. We used to have regular check-ins on my training goals, we got on well and the sessions were varied and enjoyable.

We worked together two to three times a week for five years, then in 2018 he decided to have a career change and he moved to Spain to work as a personal fitness coach at a tennis academy. When he left, I was passed to another personal trainer at my gym, but he only stayed for three months and then he moved on. This happened another couple of times – just as I got to know the new instructor, he left.

So, I decided to go it alone for a little while, but I found it difficult and I didn't have the discipline or motivation to really follow through on my training. In 2019, I met another trainer who has been absolutely brilliant. He has a plan in place to look after all of his clients in the future because he intends to have a franchised training business with other trainers, which means if he retires, moves on or is even just on holiday, there will be other trainers who can continue with me, and all of his other clients, and remain true to his ethos.

This is really important because it is very easy to start on a path, whether that's with health and fitness training or financial planning, and then be knocked off track. Knowing that there are other well-qualified and empathetic advisers in a business who can support you and help you stick to your plan is invaluable.

I would also say that it is incredibly valuable to work with a firm that encourages you to develop a relation-ship with several of its advisers because we all have our strengths and, from your perspective as a client, having a whole team of financial planners working with you can mean you get the best of everyone's skills.

For example, at my firm we have one adviser who is excellent at digging into cash flow modelling with our clients. We now conduct client meetings together, where she sets out the modelling software and we jointly run through that at the meeting with the clients. This means that not only do my clients get the benefit of her expertise in addition to mine but also that they meet a younger adviser, which may be important for longer-term succession for when I ultimately retire, and start to build a relationship with people in my wider team. As a client, you want to find not only an adviser you trust but an entire firm that looks to give you the greatest benefit and value they possibly can.

Summary

Your financial plan is important for helping you to achieve the future you want and to ultimately retire in such a way that you not only have peace of mind over your financial situation but also that you still have purpose in your life. You can use a more simplistic method of valuing and projecting your future wealth or complete a thorough cash flow modelling plan depending upon your preference.

While cash flow modelling is one aspect of financial planning, it is far from all that a good financial adviser offers as part of their service. They will also regularly update your financial plan with you and check on your progress to ensure you are on track to achieve your financial goals. Financial planning gives you a great deal of clarity about your future and can bring incredible peace of mind when you are able to see that not only do you have enough but that you have more than enough to see you through your retirement. Knowing that the adviser and firm you employ have a robust succession and servicing plan in place for you is critical and a minimum expectation for you.

I've talked a bit about the importance of a good financial planner in helping you create your financial plan, but in the final chapter I'll look at how to set up a financial support network in greater detail, as well as which professionals that might include.

Chapter 9:

Your Financial
Support Network

"Alone we can do so little; together we can do so much."

— Helen Keller

In the first chapter of this book I talked about the need for advice, service and performance to go hand-in-hand, and when you are looking to engage with a chartered financial planner, these are the three elements you want to find.

Advice is intangible – you do not physically pick the advice up and take it home with you in a shopping bag. It's not like when you buy a new car and you choose the brand you want, whether it's electric, hybrid or diesel, the size of the engine to deliver the performance you want, the colour and the interior styling. In this scenario, you hand over your £20,000, £30,000 or £40,000 to a salesperson and you drive away with a tangible product. Financial advice is not like that; you cannot physically see it. However, by buying it and following through on the advice recommendations, this intangible advice can impact the life of yourself, your family and your future generations for the better far more than the car that is standing on your driveway. Much like buying a new car, however, it isn't free.

So, the benefits of the advice you receive can take years or, in some cases, decades to materialise and it won't only be you who sees those benefits but the generations who come after you.

Service can be similarly intangible. If we come back to buying our car, you will usually want to know what kind of warranty you will have, what will happen if the car breaks down, how and when it will need to be serviced and so on. Service is just as important in the world of financial advice, particularly in this era post-Covid-19 where the service levels provided by some insurance companies and banks have dropped, in my view, substantially.

The key is to engage with a financial advice firm that provides you with a local point of contact and who can liaise with the likes of insurance companies and banks to save you those issues and the time you would otherwise spend contacting various providers and other professionals, such as doctors when it comes to dealing with health insurance. Outstanding client service should always be maintained, no matter what is happening in the world.

The final element is performance. The key to this is understanding what financial products you have, what risk you are taking with each and what realistic longer-term returns you should expect on those investments in line with their volatility and risk positioning. A good financial adviser firm will, as I mentioned in the earlier chapters, be continually monitoring the performance of the fund managers they work with to ensure they are performing in line with expectations and their mandate. You should know all of this, as well as what process is followed if a fund manager is replaced, whether that is because they are underperforming or because they are retiring. Your financial adviser should also explain how your portfolio will be rebalanced to avoid the skewing of your investment risk.

In my view, advice and service from a chartered financial planner always comes before performance, but you need all three elements to be working together to get the most out of your investments and the most out of your relationship with your adviser.

Choosing a financial adviser who is knowledgeable, takes and invests their time to get to know you and who you therefore like and trust is so important because they have an impact on all three of those areas.

How to find a financial adviser

I would recommend that you interview two or three advisers, and therefore firms, when you start looking for someone to engage with. The key things to look for are whether the adviser is genuinely interested in you as a person, and not just your money, as well as the quality of the firm.

You should also look at the reputation the firm has, the quality of its service delivery, how it manages its funds, the product range available, how long the firm has been in business and what succession plans it has in place for its advisers.

When you set out to find firms and advisers in the first instance, my advice is to speak to a variety of people. Have conversations with IFAs as well as those at restricted firms, and even speak to the banks to find out what they can offer. The best thing you can do is your own due diligence. Carry out research on the internet and interview some local firms to get an idea of the market and the quality of service and advice available in different places.

There can be some polarisation in the financial advice world around restricted and independent advisers; however, as I explained earlier, I don't believe that whether an adviser is independent or restricted is the most important quality to look for. The qualifications that an adviser holds are, in my opinion, more important. Does the adviser have the mandatory entry-level financial planning diploma, which is a level four qualification, or are they chartered, which is a level six qualification? I also have a lot of respect for certified financial planners, who have a similar level of qualification to chartered financial planners and a great deal of experience around establishing a comprehensive client financial plan itself. Certified financial planners will carry out a detailed assessment of your long-term life financial plan, which can be incredibly valuable.

Another qualification to look out for is whether a financial adviser is SOLLA registered, as I discussed in Chapter 6. The adviser you are working predominantly with might not be SOLLA registered, but is there an adviser within the firm who is and who they can refer you to if either yourself or your family will require later life advice in future? Intergenerationally, it is important to have someone who can advise you around long-term care needs and how best to prepare for those financially.

When you are looking for an adviser, I would say that qualifications should make up about 30 per cent of what you're looking for; the other 70 per cent is the person themselves (whether you like and trust them), the succession plan they have in place and that they deliver advice, service and performance, aligned with the quality of the underlying firm and its reputation.

You want to find an adviser who genuinely understands you and who will take the time to "stand in your shoes and walk around in them" to ensure they do the best they can for you in the short, medium and long term, rather than focusing on the initial fee they can earn from having you as a client.

You might also want to ask the questions: "How many clients do you currently look after and what is the maximum number you take on to reach capacity?" and: "When you do reach client capacity, who then looks after these clients and what is the handover process?" – the reason being that it is only possible to really get to know and holistically understand a finite number of clients. Can an adviser with, say, 500-plus client relationships really understand every client's goals and aspirations?

Your financial support network

It can also be helpful to find an adviser who has a well-rounded knowledge of the financial marketplace. For example, I advised clients directly and worked in the mortgage market for over two years (between 2004 and 2007) and, although I don't advise directly in this area any longer, the knowledge and experience gained has been invaluable in supporting my younger clients who might be exploring their options for their first property or their remortgage or a client looking for a buy-to-let mortgage.

You want to find a financial adviser who is aware of when to refer you for products or services that are important, but that they don't provide themselves, such as legal advice, will writing, LPA, general and home insurance, mortgage and equity release advice, taxation and accounting advice or even business consulting. Your financial adviser can connect you to other professionals who can deliver those services and, if you have chosen a financial adviser who offers excellent advice, service and performance, you can rest assured that the other people in their network are equally focused on delivering excellent advice, service and performance. This is about developing a network of knowledgeable professionals who can support every aspect of your financial life and this won't all come from one person.

I mentioned business consulting in the previous list and if you run your own business this is an area you will likely benefit from having support in. I work closely with an organisation of business growth consultants called Elephants Child, who look at all the elements that need to be in place to ensure business growth, right from the balance sheet and financials to staff recruitment, retention and the consumer supply chain. They also have a close eye on business exit planning and are very experienced with management buyouts (MBOs) and acquisitions.

I will typically work with Elephants Child when I have a client who wants a growth plan in order to expand their business or when a client is ready to consider and prepare their business for a sale and their exit, as well as to help them negotiate the right deal for their own and their staff/team's long-term sustainability.

While I have mentioned Elephants Child here because they are the firm I work with and continue to recommend to my business clients, I would say that you can form a valuable partnership with any good firm of business consultants, who can complement your financial planning and make your business stronger. The job of business consultants is to have you work "on" your business rather than only work "in" it. In essence, they enable you to see the "wood from the trees" and take valuable time out of the day-to-day running of your business to set out a plan of action with specific goals aligned to growth and exit. I was a member of Strategic Coach® from 2013 to 2018. They helped me with all aspects of my business – I cannot speak highly enough of them and, until you have experienced good business coaching and consultation, it is difficult to precisely explain their value to the business owner both personally and indeed to all business stakeholders.

The point I'd like to make here is that it's very easy to mismanage your business growth plans and ultimate business exit, especially during challenging economic times, which can have a significant negative impact both on you as a sole trader/partner or director and on the company itself. A good coach will put a growth plan in place and complement that with an exit plan. What I do, as your financial planner, is assist with your business and personal protection, as well as your pension planning, savings and investments and inheritance tax mitigation, all of which complements the business growth position and helps you have a happier and more fulfilled life.

I think of this network like a wheel with you, as the client, in the centre and the various professionals you are engaging with radiating out from there. Through my financial advice, I want to connect you to a support network of excellent professionals to deliver holistic support to you and your family throughout your life-time and beyond.

As an adviser, I know that each client has many needs and I can't possibly serve all of them, so I see it as my role to signpost and support my clients to engage with the right professionals at the right time to serve those needs. This is one of the things you should be looking for in a financial adviser.

Understanding fees associated with financial advice, both initially and on an ongoing basis

When you start checking out different firms, you will have an initial meeting with their advisers and this should typically be free of charge. However, as well as covering their client data confidentiality aspects, their polarisation (independent or restricted advice), their FCA regulation position, the FSCS protections afforded and their complaints procedure at this meeting, their complete fee schedule and structure should be fully disclosed in writing, as well as discussed and explained and your understanding confirmed.

Meeting a few advisers and firms is sensible (we are told to always get three quotes for a building job as an example) and, once you have done this and got an idea of how each of them works and whether you can see yourself developing a long-term relationship with that adviser and firm, you can consider the fees that each charges. This isn't only about how much the fees are in themselves but also what you are going to receive from a service, advice and performance perspective for that fee. Remember the maxim: "Buy cheap, buy twice."

Since 2013 and the Retail Distribution Review (RDR), financial advising firms have been forced to be completely transparent about their total fees for the financial advice their advisers provide. It is mandatory, under RDR, that a firm's fee for the "advice" element, that is both initial advice and the ongoing advice (for future advice and service reviews), is specifically distinguished from the "product and administration" element of the overall fee charged to the client. Financial advising firms will charge an initial advice fee and an ongoing advice fee for looking after and comprehensively reviewing the client's circumstances and the suitability of the products initially recommended on a continuous (defined as at least annually) basis. Firms will take those fees in different ways and, as with most things in life, fees can be negotiated by the client.

Some firms and advisers, often IFAs, will charge a fixed upfront initial advice fee (paid for by a cheque or invoice) and then usually there will be the underlying fund manager or platform fee for the underlying products and services that the adviser recommends. In this case, the adviser may also charge a fixed annual fee for the ongoing annual advice and service review of your portfolio. Other firms and advisers will charge the initial and ongoing advice fees through the products and services you take up with them via a percentage of the annual management charge.

Total fees – both initial and ongoing advice fees and product/administration fees – should all be transparently communicated to you, and you should be happy that the fees are fair to cover the service, advice and performance you receive. Under RDR, if you do not receive ongoing advice from your adviser you are able to turn off the ongoing advice fee attached to the product(s) you purchased and therefore still enjoy the product at a lower overall price (if you are paying the ongoing advice fee by fixed fee, you will not have seen your adviser so of course you will not have paid it).

So, ongoing advice from your financial adviser is arguably more important than the initial advice and recommendations you receive. Therefore, if you're not receiving the advice and service you are paying for, you can stop the ongoing advice fee the adviser firm will charge.

What should you expect to receive on an ongoing basis, at least annually, for the advice fee you are paying?

- A face-to-face (or virtual face-to-face) comprehensive review of your current circumstances, including any changes to your personal circumstances, income needs, plans, goals and aspirations.

- An update of any legislation/budgetary/taxation changes and how these changes may impact on your own situation and planning.

- An assessment of the suitability of your existing products, plans and trusts and a confirmation that they remain appropriately matched to your current circumstances.

- A review of your attitude to investment risk and the consideration of a fund/portfolio re-balance to avoid a skewing of your investment risk (this means, in effect, rebalancing your funds so that they "go back" to their original fund and asset allocations).

- Consideration of pension annual allowance usage, ISA allowances and any new advice recommendations to meet the review of your circumstantial changes as described.

Following this annual advice meeting, the discussions, recommendations and any follow-up service actions should be followed up in writing. It is worth repeating here that advice fees can be negotiated with your adviser – transparency and fairness are important.

Avoid split advice

Sometimes clients will tell me that, in addition to taking advice from me, they are going to seek advice from an IFA, a bank or another financial adviser, but I will always recommend against this kind of split advice, largely because what another adviser will recommend may either contradict or duplicate my advice. The old adage: "Too many cooks spoil the broth," is true when it comes to financial advice.

My recommendation is to engage one chartered financial planner and, if you don't trust that person to deliver that full service and advice plan, find someone you do trust. Split advice rarely works because you are going to end up with a contradiction somewhere along the line. If you apply this scenario to other areas of your life, it's like using two or three physios, or two accountants to complete your tax return. If you are considering taking this approach, I would invite you to ask yourself why. Is it because you're hedging your bets in case one of them doesn't do a good job? I would argue it's better to take your time to find someone you trust and just engage that one person.

Sometimes a prospective client says to me: "Howard, we do not want to have all of our money with your firm." My response is that actually you don't, as the fund managers we employ are external to the firm. All I do is provide you with the advice to invest into those products and thereby funds and, as we have a wide choice of managers and portfolios as well as our own discretionary fund manager I can call upon if your portfolio is very large, you have all the diversification you require – you do not need to seek another adviser for fund investment diversification; we can provide it for you.

Why engage a financial planner?

One of the simple reasons why you may want to engage a financial planner is that you have a busy life and don't want to spend your time reviewing all that is required to update your financial position, or maybe you do not particularly enjoy doing this. It might be that you simply want a second opinion about your financial situation. Or you may be the member of a couple who takes care of all the finances and you are concerned about how your partner will cope if you were to pass away. Having a financial adviser and firm you trust can therefore give you great peace of mind that your partner and family will be looked after and supported should you pass away.

Ultimately, at what point you choose to engage a financial adviser will be down to your circumstances. For most people it is whenever they realise that the benefits of engaging someone outweigh the cost of seeking that advice. I have had clients come to one of my investment seminars and many months or often years later call me to book an initial meeting because they have decided that now is the right time for them.

Most people seek face-to-face (and/or virtual) advice for all the reasons I've outlined in this book: they want to save time, save tax, build a local contact relation-ship and pass on their wealth to the next generation. One of the benefits of engaging a trusted financial adviser is getting clarity over what your magic number is for a secure retirement or financial independence and putting a plan in place to achieve that figure. You will also have someone to steer you along the seven golden rules of investment, helping you to invest the right amount of money and ensuring that it is invested in a tax-efficient way.

A financial adviser can also save you money on income tax, capital gains tax and inheritance tax. They can ensure you have the right level of income at the right time and advise you on everything from complicated financial products, such as VCTs, EIS, pensions and TIBs, to more simple products like ISAs and unit trusts.

Financial advice also runs into life advice and, to a degree, life counselling and coaching advice. I frequently find myself suggesting to my clients that they spend more money. You're only here once, so make the most of it and enjoy your time and your wealth. Often people who are very frugal and have saved all their lives will continue that into their retirement, which is why I find myself often suggesting to clients that they might spend more money and enjoy what they have worked their whole lifetime for while their health allows.

For me, this is one of the major benefits of engaging a trusted financial adviser: you have someone who sees life from your perspective, stands in your shoes and walks around in them, acts as a sounding board and who can provide a "fresh pair of eyes" to help you reflect on your position and answer any questions you have. My role is also to refer you to other professionals who can support you in whatever you decide to do next, whether that's someone to write an LPA or arrange for you to remortgage.

If you are particularly interested in your finances and financial planning in general, you may decide to do some or all of what I've talked about in this book yourself. If you decide to do that, I would simply ask you to be very careful because the consequences of getting something wrong, particularly with a document like your will or LPA, can be severe for both you and your family. Remember that not only will a professional have the knowledge and skills to avoid mistakes, but their firm will also have professional indemnity insurance you can rely on and so financially recompense you should any issues arise in future.

Having read this book, you may fall into the camp of people who believe they can do everything themselves. However, I will make one final point in this area and that is that you don't know what you don't know. Why not engage someone who has 30-plus years of experience in this area? They might only be able to help you with one element of your financial plan, but that one element could save you tens of thousands of pounds, which would make them more than worth their fees.

Summary

A financial support network stretches beyond a trusted financial adviser. This is a good starting point, and ideally the person you engage should be able to help you build that network of other trusted professionals who can provide the advice, service and performance in all the areas I've discussed in this book that can have an impact on your financial life.

Finding someone you trust is the key to getting the right support network in place, so don't be afraid to interview multiple financial advisers and ask the questions I have outlined here. This will help you find someone who is the right fit for you and for your family in the future.

All aspects of the fees you pay for the advice and the underlying products should be transparently and clearly explained to you so that you understand them and perceive them as fair, both initially and on a continuous basis.

Conclusion

I started this book by discussing the importance of the three expectations of advice, service and performance, and hopefully you can now see how those three elements can come together in a relationship with a financial adviser that will provide you with long-term support in multiple areas of your life, as well as supporting other generations in your family.

Although all three of these expectations are very important, advice and service are marginally more important than performance alone in my opinion; however, all three should complement one another.

The seven golden rules of investing are essential to consider when you are making any decisions around investments, whether that is in relation to investment funds or some of the other kinds of investments I discussed in Chapter 7.

As a reminder, the seven golden rules are:

1. Never borrow to invest.

2. Keep enough cash – but not too much!!! – and find the best market cash interest rates.

3. Invest primarily to beat inflation.

4. Diversify across all five main asset classes in order to minimise investment risk and volatility.

5. Invest for the longer term and seek to involve your beneficiaries in the discussions where and when you are comfortable.

6. Find the best provider to manage your capital and to provide you with top-quality advice and service.

7. Never invest in anything you do not fully understand and do not attempt to "time" the market.

If you stick to these seven golden rules it is very difficult to go wrong with your investments because you will always have enough cash, you will have invested in vehicles that suit your appetite for risk and you will be focusing on the long term to achieve your goals.

In Part 2, I talked about several elements that complement a strong financial plan but that aren't necessarily financial in nature, such as wills and LPA. These are absolutely vital and are a cornerstone of good financial planning because without them you are leaving a very difficult legacy for your beneficiaries. This is why intergenerational advice is so important.

I also talked about inheritance tax and how, with initial and ongoing advice and careful planning, it can largely be avoided or at the very least reduced. When it comes to inheritance tax, the key is to regularly review your position (at least annually) and to engage with the next generation. You want to make sure that you understand how your position might alter with changes in legislation, as well as knowing how it can change as you accumulate more wealth.

Advice is incredibly important when it comes to pensions and your retirement fund. While financial advice and service is useful and important in the pre-retirement accumulation stage, it becomes absolutely vital at the post-retirement decumulation stage of your life, especially when you are considering options such as a phased or staggered retirement.

Later life advice, a bit like wills and LPA, is important not only from a financial perspective but also from an emotional and family perspective. Having someone you trust who can guide you through what can be a difficult journey both emotionally and financially is incredibly valuable. This is about making sure that those four pillars of your later life (exercise, socialisation, nutrition and finances) are taken care of to enable you to live as full a life as possible for as long as possible. While a financial adviser might focus on the financial side of things, a SOLLA-registered adviser will also be in a position to signpost you to other services and professionals who can support at this stage.

In the final chapter of Part 2, I talked about alternative investment options, my sixth asset class, which ties in with golden rule number four about diversifying, but I also wanted to share some of the pitfalls to watch out for if you are considering alternative investments like whisky, art, gold and penny shares. It's also important to understand the difference between appreciating and depreciating assets so that you understand what you are buying (see golden rule number seven!).

Having a good financial plan can be incredibly valuable, although not everyone will need one. However, one of the advantages of working with a trusted financial adviser is access to the likes of cash flow modelling software that can help you map out your financial future, set goals and plan for different scenarios.

This is where having a solid financial support network becomes very useful and, when you are looking for a financial adviser, I would suggest looking for someone who is well-connected and who takes a holistic approach to financial planning, as they will help you to find other professionals who can support you on your journey. Fees are obviously important and transparency is the key here. Do your due diligence and investigate a few firms and advisers before making your decision.

Remember to also look for someone with a chartered or certified financial planning qualification over and above an adviser with a standard diploma because the advice quality and depth of their knowledge/experience is likely to be higher.

If you have found what I have shared in this book useful, and feel that my firm might be the right one for you, please contact me to arrange an initial meeting, discuss your situation and see if we are a good fit for one another.

You might feel that this book has provided you with useful information that makes you feel more confident about doing your own financial planning. If you are set on this course then I wish you well, although I would simply say that with a good adviser all you need to commit is an hour or two a year to staying on track with your financial plan, so if you feel the DIY route will be too much work for you, please get in touch with us.

Overall, I hope the book has afforded you a greater understanding of money, how it can be grown longer term and enjoyed and also how it can be best passed on.

You can organise either a virtual or face-to-face meeting with me, with no cost or obligation to use my services, by contacting my office on 0191 3055246 or emailing me on howard.mccain@icloud.com.

You can also contact me and find more information about the financial planning services my firm offers at www.howardmccain.co.uk.

About the Author

Born in Sunderland in 1965, Howard targeted a career in finance from early school age and in 1982 joined NatWest Bank in South Shields. He completed his chartered banking associateship in 1993 and it was in that year that he was appointed as a financial adviser at the Gateshead branch of the bank.

In 1994, he chose the management route and progressed through various first and second line financial advisory management roles with NatWest.

Disillusioned with the bank's relentless sales culture, he made his one and only career move to St. James's Place Wealth Management in 2004. He then passed his Chartered Financial Planner Associateship and Fellowship qualifications by 2012 and his SOLLA qualification in 2016.

In 2020, having run his own business, Howard McCain Wealth Associates, for 16 years, he moved to Sovereign Wealth, a Principal Partner Practice of St. James's Place Wealth Management.

Since 2013, Howard has raised, with company matching and supported by his clients and St. James's Place colleagues, over £150,000 for the St. James's Place Charitable Foundation via overseas mountain treks to Scotland, Italy, Spain, Montenegro and, in 2017 and 2018, to Nepal where two schools have been built near Kathmandu to help support those affected by the devastating 2015 earthquake.

Married to Gill, a teacher and lead soprano cornet player with Durham Mineworkers' Brass Band, who currently works with him in the new business, he has two sons, Alex, 24, who is also a teacher and a karate black belt, and Euan, 14, who loves his football and plays at the Sunderland AFC Foundation of Light – they also have a much loved cocker spaniel, Fergus.

Outside of work, table tennis, tennis, fly fishing and sharing the joy (but mainly the pain) of watching his beloved Sunderland AFC occupy much of his time, as well as family time spent at their cottage in Weardale.

Printed in Great Britain
by Amazon

80564129R00231